BEHIND THE
☆☆☆☆☆☆☆☆☆☆☆☆☆☆☆☆☆☆
RANK

VOL 2

BEHIND THE

☆☆☆☆☆☆☆☆☆☆☆☆☆☆☆☆☆

RANK

VOL 2

LILA HOLLEY

purposely
created
PUBLISHING

BEHIND THE RANK VOLUME 2

Published by Purposely Created Publishing Group™

Copyright © 2018 Lila Holley

Printed in the United States of America

ISBN: 978-1-947054-62-2

Special discounts are available on bulk quantity purchases by book clubs, associations and special interest groups. For details email: sales@publishyourgift.com or call (888) 949-6228.

For information logon to:
www.PublishYourGift.com

TABLE OF CONTENTS

HEALING IS A PROCESS

FROM UGLY SCAR TO BEAUTY MARK

FOREWORD

As a person who never served but comes from a family with an extensive history of service in the military, I am honored to share what Behind the Rank means to me. My name is Portia Chandler and I am the fourth of five children. All of my uncles (my dad's brothers) enlisted and many of their children (my first cousins) served in some branch of the military. My older brother enlisted in the Air Force and my older sister (who enlisted straight out of high school) served and retired from the United States Army. My sister and I are exactly 10 months and 13 days apart. (Side Note: either my mom was a fast one or my dad couldn't wait any longer). Everyone believed that we were twins. We did absolutely everything together. My mother often dressed us alike and combed our hair the exact same. Even though she was older than me, we graduated from high school together. The day she left for the Army my heart broke. I didn't even know she was thinking about enlisting. We had never been apart in our lives. To be honest, it felt like betrayal. Why didn't she tell me? It was her first independent decision.

The first couple of months of her Army career were very hard for the both of us. What she didn't know was that I was expecting my first child while she was leaving for Basic Training. We wrote letters every day during Basic Training, and we cried for the entire 20 minutes of her first call home. We tried to encourage one another to keep pressing forward. She wanted to quit Basic Training and my first trimester had me seriously wondering what I had gotten myself into. We prayed for one another's struggles and I prayed that the distance between us and the uncomfortable situations we were experiencing would be over soon, and they were. I gave birth to a healthy, handsome baby boy, she graduated from Basic Training and went on to her first assignment, and we both began to chart our course into adulthood.

Fast forward 21 years later as I stand at an induction ceremony for my first born son. He has decided to take a career path similar to my sister's. I was heartbroken. During a time where America had elected a celebrity as president and rumors of wars were being discussed around the clock, this was the last thing I expected to have to deal with. But, I did what any mother would have done, I let him make his own decisions. I was built for this, after all, I had been through this before. I learned how to detach in a healthy manner in order to heal.

The beautiful thing about having siblings, parents, and children serving in the military is that you learn an entirely different definition of freedom and sacrifice. To me, freedom and sacrifice go hand in hand because I know the sacrifice I faced as a sibling and now as a mother of an Armed Forces service member. I know that because of their service, I am afforded a wonderful life full of freedoms to pursue my dreams and desires. I am extremely proud of all my family members who have served, especially my sister and now my son. I believe that civilians, like myself, must love enough to let go and trust enough to hold on for your loved ones to eventually return to you safely. So for me, the Behind the Rank story is:

- ❯ The story of courage to take the oath. The oath my sister, son, and so many of my family members have taken.

- ❯ The story of service. To selflessly give of oneself to one's country even during uncertain times.

- ❯ The story of love. The love of family to support each other even when we don't always understand or agree with each other's decisions.

My prayer is that everyone, everywhere will buy this book to better understand the dynamics of all parties involved with those who unselfishly serve their country.

Portia Chandler
CEO, PA & Associates
askportia.com
iam@portiachandler.com

BEHIND THE RANK, VOLUME 2

Well, we're back to continue this incredible series by sharing the stories Behind the Rank of more extraordinary military women! In *Behind the Rank, Volume 1*, we shared stories from 29 courageous military women that focused on: Duty to Self, Duty to Serve, and Duty to Family. We enjoyed learning more about the plight of the military woman as they shared delicate details of their lives and allowed themselves to be vulnerable for the sake of leaving readers with a message of hope. We salute them for their transparency and sincerity as they voiced their lessons learned from the challenges they faced throughout their military careers and lives.

Now, here we are in Volume 2 with 16 new co-authors bearing their souls, sharing their stories, their lessons learned, and more messages of hope. Get ready! This book is sure to inspire as you, once again, get the opportunity to look Behind the Rank. I always say that the story of the military woman is layered—the good, the not so good, and the down-right ugly. Camouflaged Sisters books allow you to look at all layers of our stories, in our own voices, as military women—always honoring our service.

Journey with us as we go further Behind the Rank, diving deeper into Duty to Self. The word duty means an obligation or action someone is required to perform. While self is defined as the essential being that distinguishes someone from others. Our *obligation* with the Camouflaged Sisters brand, books, and movement is to value the voice of *distinguished people*—military women who, for so long, felt they did not have a voice or that their stories did not matter. Diving deeper into Duty to Self is our way of giving value to their voices and honor to their service.

Military women are indeed a unique breed of women. Having taken an oath of duty, they now belong to a special sisterhood. As these courageous women share their stories about their journey, you will find that the road to Duty to Self required them to deal with:

- ❯ Wounds: pain or an injury of sorts that occurred during their military career and lives (not necessarily a physical wound but a wound none the less).

- ❯ Healing: the process of restoration and repair that results in a scar.

- ❯ Beauty: lessons learned that now allow them to look at that scar as a beauty mark.

Many women can relate to having visible and invisible scars from their life's journey, especially military women who have the scars that serving in the military can leave behind. Think about it, a scar indicates that an injury occurred and healing has since taken place. As you read these stories, you will see that these women had to deal with the injury of being wrongly accused, denied and delayed promotions and awards, confinement, and further rejection from the very system they took an oath to serve. But through it all, they held on to their faith and remained positive throughout the journey. It is this faith that allows them to heal and now look at their scars as beauty marks.

Lila H.

WOUNDED
BUT NOT
DESTROYED

THE EMOTIONS OF SERVICE

☆ ☆ ☆ ☆ ☆

LILA HOLLEY

The Emotional Story

I'm so proud to be a US Army woman Veteran, and I'm always looking for the opportunity to share my story with anyone who will listen. While sharing is comfortable for me, this is not the case for many women who served in the military. Many are still reluctant to share their experiences due to the painful memories associated with their service; but, that's a conversation for another time.

As for me, I share my story freely. I share what us Veterans call "war stories," lessons learned, and humor-laced stories from my military career. While I have deployed in support of combat operations during my military career, many of the stories I choose to share don't focus on my combat experience. Many of the stories I share are often centered on the emotions of serving in the military, being a woman who served, and being an African American woman who served.

I must admit, I enjoy sharing my war stories, especially with other Veterans. During my deployments, I walked away with many lessons learned that made me a better leader, Soldier, and analyst. I had a wonderful career, served with some amazing leaders and Soldiers that inspired me, and traveled the world. I most definitely don't mind sharing the details of that. But, the main reason I share my story is because stories like mine are not in the history books, and if I don't tell the story, who will tell it for me? More importantly, who will *accurately* tell it.

My story is unique and has many layers. The piece of my story that I enjoy sharing the most is about the emotions of serving in the military. I know you're thinking, "What do you mean the emotions?" Yes, the emotions of service. This is the part of the story you don't hear about often, yet it remains an important part of the journey of those serving and those who have served in the military, especially women. Let's be honest, the current political atmosphere in America is pretty intense. Racial tension, hate, and anger are at an all-time high. But, I still believe that the US is the best country on the planet and it gives women the most opportunities, especially women in the military. Women are afforded the opportunity to serve in numerous roles, especially with combat jobs now available to us. Women are literally breaking glass ceilings and making history. Even today we still read about someone being the "first woman to _____." You can fill in the blank.

Regardless, there are still many misconceptions about women in the military or why women choose the military as a career. Some misconceptions are:

> ❯ All the women in the military have been sexually assaulted.

> ❯ These women had no other career options or ran out of options.

> ❯ They're all damaged and will likely end up homeless or unemployed when they leave the military.

Obviously, these ideas are untrue. I equate this type of thinking to people who just don't know what they don't know. Keep in mind that according to Department of Veterans Affairs data, only 1 percent of the US population serves in the active military. Factor in Veterans, and that number rises to about 7 percent of Americans having served in the military at some point in their lives. That's a small portion of our population, so I normally give people a pass when they jump to a wrong conclusion or make an ignorant statement about women in the military. They get one mess up, then I'm going in and sharing my story to right the wrong misconceptions.

Emotional Beginning

My story began with a desire to serve. It just so happens that my desire led me to the military after taking Junior ROTC classes in high school. I really enjoyed Junior Reserve Officer

Training Corps (JROTC) and surprised myself as I grew into a great leader within my class. I knew after the first year of high school that I wanted to pursue a career in the military. However, this was an ambitious goal to have because I was not what you would call an ideal recruit for a military recruiter. Yes, my test scores were high and I had completed two years of JROTC, but despite all of that I came with baggage. After finding out I was a teenage single mother, the Air Force recruiter back-pedaled about my options and talked so badly about the process of joining with a child that all my hopes and dreams went right out the window. The only thing he didn't say was, "We don't want you." But, his actions most definitely said it all.

I was devastated. I thought my chance of joining the military was shot. That is until I walked out of his office and right into the Army recruiter waiting outside. I know he saw the look of defeat on my face. Why else was he prompted to ask me, "What did he say to you?" I told him, and I even shared what my test scores were and the fact that I was a single mother. He smiled and invited me into his office. And the rest, as they say, is history! I served honorably for 22 years in the US Army as an intelligence analyst, reaching the rank of Staff Sergeant before transitioning to Warrant Officer and retiring as a Chief Warrant Officer Four, all thanks to that recruiter who took the time to listen to my emotional story and walk me through the process of enlisting.

My military career began with high emotions. And, as I look back over my 22 years of service, I've had significant moments throughout my career where I rode the emotional roller coaster. So, fasten your seatbelt and join me on this ride...

The Guilt of Service

It was the 90's and the US military was engulfed in peacekeeping operations in the Balkans which involved Troops being deployed to Bosnia, Croatia, Kosovo, Macedonia, and parts of Turkey. I received word that I would be deploying to Bosnia in support of ongoing operations in the region. I was both excited and nervous as a newly promoted Chief Warrant Officer Two. Despite all the emotions, I knew this would be a great opportunity to learn and grow as an analyst. As a single mother in the military, this meant that I had to kick into action my Family Care Plan (the contingency plan for the care of my son in the event I had to deploy). I was comforted knowing that my family would step in and help me out when needed, and this was definitely a time of need. So, my brother stepped up and volunteered to come help me out for the six months I was scheduled to deploy. He would stay with my son, in my house, and handle any situation that came up.

With everything in place, I set off on my deployment to Bosnia. It was truly a great learning environment as I worked with some amazing leaders, including several Warrant Officers. Bosnia was where I first met my mentor, CW4 (Retired) Amanda Randolph. It was a good experience for my first deployment and I was grateful for the opportunity. Time was ticking away as I marked off the days on my calendar, anticipating the day I would return home. And speaking of home, things were going well. My brother, Damon, was really handling being a "parent" well, considering he is not that much older than my son (just eight years to be exact).

Everything was going along just fine. Then, one day I made a phone call home and found out that my son's friend had been killed in a car accident. Oh my goodness! Here I was thousands of miles away and my son was dealing with death for the first time! All I wanted to do was hug him tight, but all I could do was give him mere words of comfort. I felt like any efforts I made fell completely short of what he really needed at that very moment. I felt that what he needed was me, my presence, my hug, and a kiss on his forehead from his mom. But, I wasn't there to give it to him. No matter how much I tried to encourage him, the guilt of not being there grew. And, you know what? I'm not even sure how he felt about me not being there in that moment. All I knew was how I felt and how I beat myself up with guilt. Again, my brother stepped up in my absence and comforted my son. He even escorted him to the memorial service in remembrance of his friend. I felt like I had failed my son because as his mother it was my job to protect him and help him maneuver through life. I should have been the one there to help him work through his feelings. But duty called, and I was not there.

The Shame of Service

The year was 2011 and I was preparing to host my family as they traveled to Kentucky to help me celebrate the end of my military career. What a joyous occasion! The stories, the memories, the accolades, the awards, the laughs, the tears, the party. What a way to end it all! Yes, I was truly ready for retirement. I mean, I had served my 22 years. It was time! So, why was I crying like a baby while signing my leave form to make my transition from active duty Soldier to Retiree? I couldn't understand it!

My emotions during transition were all over the place. I was excited, anxious, glad, sad, relieved, abandoned, confused, and angry just to name a few. I was at a loss because I did not expect all of that. I figured the emotional outbursts would subside as I continued through the transition process, so I brushed it off. We prepared to move closer to our family in New York upon my retirement because I felt like that was where I needed to be. We were excited at the thought of being close to our family on a regular basis. But even then, I found myself feeling some strong emotions about moving back to my hometown after being away for so long. Again, I brushed those feelings off and marched forward with our relocation plan.

I guess I can say my transition was moving forward, at least I hadn't attempted to put on a uniform for months. But the emotions were still there, like a stench lingering in the air. I worked hard to hide them and the impact they were having on me. I would wake up, jump on the treadmill, watch the morning news, and smile. I would spend time with my 92-year-old grandmother and smile. (Ok, Grandma truly did make me smile. You can't spend time with a witty 90+-year-old woman and *not* smile!) I remained quiet when I wanted to yell or voice my opinion. I was simply not myself. I worked hard to become who I thought everyone else wanted me to be—not even knowing who I was or who I wanted to be during this transition. It was a tough time for me and I suffered in complete silence.

Then it happened. My husband saw a change in me as I struggled to hide one emotion—anger. I became this angry person. I can't even say I was "angry Lila" because my behavior was so out of character. One day he called me out. "What's going on with you? You're not the same loving woman I married." His words opened the floodgates. I broke down. I confessed that I had been crying myself to sleep at night and that I really didn't understand what I was feeling or going through. I wondered if this emotional rollercoaster ride I had been suffering through was normal. Then I said it, "I think I need help."

Although I felt the weight of the world lifted off my shoulders during our conversation, I was still very emotional. I felt ashamed and frustrated with myself. For crying out loud, I was a combat Veteran. I took Troops to war and brought them home safely! Yet, here I was crying in my pillow at night because I *missed the military*. Really? If I could, I would have shaken some damn sense into myself and yelled, "Girl, get yourself together!" Unfortunately, it was not as simple as stepping off the emotional rollercoaster.

Emotions Running High

"Who are you?"

"I'm Chief Holley, a Soldier, a leader, a wife, a mother, a daughter…"

"No, who are *you*?"

"Lady, didn't you hear me? I just told you who I am. I'm Chief Holley!" I thought to myself before asking, "What do you mean?"

This was the conversation that helped me start the next chapter of my life's journey. In that initial counseling session, I discovered a lot about myself—mainly that I had a piss poor system for processing my emotions, it was literally nonexistent. It didn't start off like that. No, over the years I grew into that "calm under pressure leader," stepping on my emotions with my combat boots for the sake of the mission and to be that calming presence in the midst of chaos, or simply because stepping on them was easier than dealing with them. It was during transition that I realized this tactic, while useful in stressful situations, was not healthy over the long haul and I had to make a change.

If you find yourself riding an emotional rollercoaster during your transition, just know that this is a normal response to a life transition and you will make it through just like the rest of us old Veterans. Now, I am not saying that as you work through this process you will wake up one day and all these crazy emotions will disappear. Sorry, it's not going to happen like that. But the days will get better. I will leave you with three tools that helped me push through:

1. Be honest about what you're feeling. Do not keep it bottled up inside. There is no honor in suffering in silence.

2. Ask for help. I know the military does not prepare us to be vulnerable, but I found that when I opened my mouth and asked many were willing to help.

3. Use the resources available to you. I will be honest, in my 22 years of military service I *never* used mental health services. I'm not saying that I didn't need them, I likely did, I'm just saying that I didn't use them until I transitioned. Using those services catapulted my forward progression through transition.

Today, my emotions continue to run high, and what a rollercoaster ride it has been. I'm riding on the joy of life, love of family, pride of service, honor as a Veteran, and value as a woman Veteran! You got this! Keep pushing because the other side is beautiful!

GIVE VOICE TO "IT"
SO YOU CAN LIVE

☆ ☆ ☆ ☆ ☆

MARSHA S. MARTIN

Scared to Say the Words

"Tell your story. You can change lives," you say. What if I tell you I am ashamed to give voice to the ugly truth that takes cover behind this caramel, brown-eyed beauty? What if I tell you that the fear of telling my story paralyzes me? What if I tell you I get shell-shocked at the mere thought of being rejected a second time by the very organization, the United States Army, and the very people, my fellow US citizens, whom I took an oath to support and defend against all enemies? What if I tell you I am genuinely afraid of what they will think of me and what they will say about me after I tell my truth? What if I tell you I CAN'T?

For years I battled against a relentless enemy that had no tangible form, yet it had plenty of substance that consumed nearly all the available space that remained in my tattered conscience. I struggled against the unforgiving reality that sooner or later, ready or not, scared or confident, I would one day have to reveal the real reason I left the US Army. I avoided exposing the details of my abrupt departure from active military service; but, in this sixth year since the reality set in, it came face to face with me and a decision had to be made.

During that dark phase in my life, I embraced God and His kingdom lifestyle and became extremely close to the Holy Spirit who I address as my Counselor. I consulted with Him about the situation. I tell you I put up a pretty good defense as to why I should not share my story. However, God in His stern but compassionate way responded, "Give voice to it so you can live. I need you to break the silence. The silence is the thing that has you in a constant state of wanting and needing to exhale from a deep breath taken years ago, but you can't." I told Him, "I do talk." His response was: "Yes, you do. But, there is a difference between talking and giving voice to that thing that will not allow you to move forward i.e., failed dreams, a failed marriage, loss of a loved one, loss of a job, disappointment, and betrayal. Talking is surface. In this phase you tend to tell people what you think they want to hear and it only brings about a change. But when you give voice to that thing, you go to the root of the problem, it brings about a transformation, and you open yourself up to be restored." He further explained that giving voice to it so you can live is simply being able to share your truth with complete clarity by coming to terms with what you have done and what you have been through while getting delivered, transformed, and restored. I, of course, was not excited about the decision I had to make. But, before I agreed, I asked God if He could walk me through the process. He responded, "The answer is already in you, give voice to it so you can live." Though disappointed, I agreed.

I've got to tell you, immediately after that I started having feelings I thought I had become hardened to. My heart grew heavy. My eyes watered. It seemed like the more I tried to fight back the tears the faster they flowed. Tears that connected to thoughts. Thoughts that opened painful memories. Memories from my time in the US Army serving as a dutiful Soldier. Memories of the awful choices I made and the way I felt when I realized that my time as an honorable Soldier would soon be finished. As those thoughts overtook my mind, tears flooded my soul like the first rain of a hurricane tearing across a deserted beach. This time, there was no place to hide. Although I had many years of practice, this time there was no longer a way to suppress the painful thoughts and the even more painful decision that had to be made and carried out. It was time to finally deal with the levees that had been holding back Hurricane Marsha.

I was immediately reminded of all the painful emotions I had suffered over the preceding years: anger, loneliness, self-loathing. And those were among the easiest ones to deal with. The hardest part was dealing with the individuals who benefited from my downfall and those who I thought would support me in a time of real crisis but turned their backs on me. They went out of their way to avoid interacting with me unless it was mandated by blood or station. It was as if I had become a black sheep, left alone to navigate an emotional minefield. And there were no Army regulations, no field manuals, no special training, and definitely no fellow Soldiers that could prepare me for the journey I was about to take.

My Voice

Unlike many of my fellow sisters and brothers in uniform, I departed the US Army as a disgrace. Tuesday, November 24, 2009, was a day that rocked my world. Having only two days left before Thanksgiving that year, I should have been focused on prepping a big family dinner; unfortunately, turkey, dressing, and cranberry sauce were not the only things filling my plate. Instead, on that day, my attorney was going over my speaking points with me, hopefully to be used as leverage for me in my court-martial.

On November 24, 2009, I, Marsha S. Martin, was tried and convicted in a Military Court- Marital on a charge of defrauding the United States government of $274,000.00. Yes, you read right. I was convicted of defrauding the federal government of two hundred seventy-four thousand dollars. For that conviction, I had to:

- spend 34 months in a stockade
- forfeit all pay and allowance

- suffer a reduction in pay grade (E-6 to E-1), and

- accept a bad conduct discharge

While serving that sentence, I came to appreciate several crucial lessons. One is that in every downfall there are at least two choices to be weighed: (1) stay down or (2) get up. For many years, I chose to stay down. And within that time, I endured just about every trying thing a downfall had to offer. Disappointment. Disbelief. Disgrace. Self-Doubt. Each one a part of the unforgiving knowledge that I had failed on such a monumental level. It was a failure I wore like and ugly badge of honor.

No one knew my internal struggle. If the situation called for it, I could talk victory and I had nearly perfected looking like it too. Yet, my soul was not at rest and my spirit was not at ease.

I longed for one person to look in my eyes and see what I was ashamed to give voice to. I needed just one person to say, "I see it, Marsha. I see what you're going through, and I am here to walk with you as you fight for your life. I am here for you." That person never came.

I'll spare you many of the details, but in March 2015, I decided that mere change was no longer enough for me. I needed to be *transformed*. I needed a new way of thinking about what's most important in my life. And I needed the strength to do what I knew had to be done.

It didn't take long for me to realize that I had become my own worst enemy. I had become the factor that was keeping me from living a life of freedom; so, it was only natural that I started the transformation by dealing squarely with me.

The Formula

So, citing irreconcilable differences, I served divorce papers to the disappointed, disgraced, failed me. Then, I began to educate myself on a new way of looking at and living through this thing called life. It has been an amazing reclamation project. Now when disappointment, disgrace, and self-doubt rear their ugly heads, I firmly resist them and they retreat.

So, what did I do to get through that time in my life? How was I able to move forward? Although the steps below seem simple, they really challenged me to change my thinking and move forward. They forced me every day to not allow the mistakes of my past to weigh me down or keep me from pushing forward to greater.

1. Get a mentor

   No matter what you go through, everyone needs a go-to person. A mentor makes the transformation process easier. You need to make sure that person is not personally invested in you. I find that sometimes it's easy to tell your story to a stranger. I say that because when they know you personally, they tend to cater to you versus being unbiased and truthful. This person needs to be able to pour into you so you can receive guidance.

2. Identify talking versus having a voice

   Talking represents a mask, it's giving the illusion of change. This means that you are really just giving people what you think they want to hear. Giving it voice represents transformation, which gets to the root of that thing you are embarrassed about. When you are in a situation where you have to decide if you should wear the mask or take it off, that moment is not one to be rushed. In that very moment, you must take your time before you react. Ask yourself, "Am I ready to just be perceived as changed or do I want to be transformed?" Take the time to consult your mentor and really think about if you're ready to move forward to be transformed and fully delivered from that thing that's kept you in bondage.

3. Make a decision

   You have the mentor, you've given a voice to it, now you must figure out what to do with all this information. Once you've given a voice to that thing that haunts you, it is time to make a decision about what you are going to do next. This step, in my opinion, is the most important. You have to decide where to go from here. To just recognize the situation is not enough. You have to position yourself to look forward to greater things. This means changing your mindset and realizing that the story does get better. You have the ability to start a new chapter. The canvas is ready to be written on.

For example, I was at a church event when I gave voice to my ugly truth. After I released it, I was full of joy and floating on cloud nine. When I arrived home, the reality that I had just exposed my secret set in. What do I do now? A flood of thoughts, negative and positive, consumed me. I shut off the voices in my head, and that night I purposed in my heart that I would live and not die. I reminded myself that the Spirit of God dwelled on the inside of me and that greatness was within me. I have been parked there ever since.

I share my decision-making moment with you, not so you can do what I did, but as a blueprint instead. You will know the exact moment and time to give voice to your truth, just embrace it when it arrives.

4. Take action

    Steps three and four go hand in hand. Immediately after you make a decision, action will have to follow it. You have to move out with purpose. You go from the vision board or words in a journal to taking action. A perfect example would be me co-author-ing this book. Breaking that silence has unleashed a woman in me I never knew existed.

Be vigilant in this action step because this is when people sometimes become stagnant. If you are not careful, you will get yourself all excited about what you want to do, how you're going to do it, who you're going to talk to, and how you're going to start getting these things done; but, then you will allow fear, laziness, procrastination, other people's thoughts about you, and even your own thoughts about you to get the best of you. Then, you don't move. It is important that you do it. That you do move. Don't get stuck because that is a hard place to get out of. Once you figure out what you want to do, take action immediately.

The key point to take away from this is that in November 2009, after suffering a major personal downfall, I chose to stay down. For nearly six years, I let that decision rule my thoughts and actions. However, in March 2015, I chose to get up and now that decision rules everything in my life. I believe that downfall was designed to destroy me. I know for sure that it could have destroyed me. But, blessed by God, supported by family, and armed with the righteous understanding that I must never give up on myself—I persevered.

You can persevere, too. You must.

THE COURAGE TO LIVE

☆ ☆ ☆ ☆ ☆

JACQUELINE NICOLE TYES

"Too many of us are not living our dreams
because we are living our fears."

—*Les Brown*

Other Than Honorable

My father is a Vietnam Veteran. As a child, my biggest dream was to serve in the military just like my father did. That is why I joined the United States Navy at the age of 17, immediately after graduating from high school. I successfully made it through boot camp and job training and then I was off to my first duty station. Within my first year, I received a three-day liberty pass for being a squared away Sailor, which meant that I always had a flawless and perfectly ironed uniform and spit-shined shoes. I also received an acceptance letter from the Broadened Opportunity for Officer Selection and

Training Program (BOOST). The BOOST Program provided extensive training to prepare enlisted Sailors for entering a Naval Officer Commissioning program, and I got accepted. Wow! That was a major accomplishment for me, especially so early in my career. My first year in the Navy was impressive. I was well on my way to a promising 20-year career, so I thought.

Unfortunately, in my second year I was injured. As a result of my injury, I was put on limited duty (LIMDU) pending a medical discharge. At my Command, my LIMDU status resulted in heightened discriminatory treatment from my superiors. This made me angry and bitter. However, instead of reacting to and reciprocating their negative behaviors, I maintained my dignity, integrity, and self-respect by responding in a way that not only protected my reputation, but also my honorable discharge. I felt that the challenges I faced were meant to break my spirit and diminish my self-esteem. The racism and the sexism were nothing like I had ever seen or experienced before in my life. It was traumatic. I felt as though I was being singled out and I felt alone. I was continuously mistreated by the highest-ranking members of my Command. I did not feel as though I had many options. So, instead of complaining I remained silent and did my job.

It felt like I was in Captain's Mast (non-judicial punishment) every other week. The charges brought against me were unfounded. Each time I was wrongfully sentenced, it was more severe than the time before. The first time I was sentenced to restriction on the boat for 15 days, then it was 15 days restriction with 15 days extra duty, then I endured 30 days restriction with 30 days extra duty, then it was 45 days restriction with 45 days extra duty. The next time at Captain's Mast, I was reduced in rank, which significantly reduced my paycheck making it impossible for me to pay my bills. Thankfully, I was able to receive financial assistance from one of my shipmates to sustain me during my hardship.

The second to last time in Captain's Mast landed me three days bread and water in the brig (confinement). Yes, three days of only bread and water. My Executive Officer (XO) and Master-at-Arms (MA) were determined to get me kicked out of the Navy with an other than honorable or dishonorable discharge. I was subjected to this mistreatment at the tender age of 19 for no reason other than being an intelligent, driven, black female on limited duty, preparing to be medically separated from the military due to an injury. My XO and MA told me to my face on several occasions that because I am a woman, I did not deserve to be in their Navy, I did not deserve a medical discharge, and I would end up working at Burger King. My last time at Captain's Mast concluded with my discharge from the Navy with an other than honorable discharge. I was devastated! I felt ashamed. My superiors got their wish. I was back at home unsure of what to do next.

Suffering in Silence

After being home for a few months, I received a call from the Bureau of Naval Personnel informing me that there was an error with my discharge. They asked if I wanted to accept my discharge or come in for another board, this time with people outside of my previous Command. I opted to have another board. I was reinstated in the Navy and sent back to the same Command with my tormentors. At my next board, my Command was unable to produce evidence that I did anything wrong and I was reinstated to my limited duty status and on my way yet again to a medical discharge.

My three long years spent in the United States Navy, though met with innumerable challenges, were the best years of my life. There were many days I wanted to go on an unauthorized absence. Other days, I wanted to fight back. Even though I felt powerless, I was determined to come out on top. I am not a quitter. I had persevered up to that point in my life, so with that in mind, every challenge was confronted with a calculated response. I was determined not to be defeated by anyone or any circumstance. However, this was not an easy task. As the months slowly passed, all I thought about was getting out of the Navy. I was sad about my premature discharge and about the way that I was being treated at my duty station.

I have held on to this part of my life since 1996. I told myself that I was okay. But, in retrospect, I was living in fear of disappointment and shame. I was fearful of appearing weak.

I felt completely alone. It felt as though I was the only one that ever dealt with this sort of situation. I didn't trust anyone with this painful memory, so I developed trust issues. For many years, I was unaware that by refusing to deal with my feelings surrounding this experience, I was allowing it to affect my life negatively. It affected the way that I lived and the decisions that I made. I buried myself in my work, I was not very social, I made poor decisions, and I was a tad reckless. Needless to say, I was not myself and I didn't even realize it. I was unknowingly suffering in silence from PTSD and depression. For too many years following my discharge, I lived in fear. I was fearful of being anything other than normal, so I wore a smile to mask my pain.

Transitioning back into civilian life was a challenge for me even after only serving for three years, especially with the extra baggage. The pain I was feeling on the inside, in addition to my injuries sustained while serving, heavily impacted my daily life. I had no idea what my new career path would be. I was unsure of how I would attain the skills needed for this new career. There were so many uncertainties, but I had to adjust my goals and reconstruct my plans. Life as I knew it had changed forever.

Lessons Learned

My experience in the US Navy was the most challenging yet the most rewarding experience in my lifetime. I met lifelong friends and gained invaluable skills that can only come from time served in the military. My experience taught me a great deal about myself and about life. In going through that experience, I learned that the way a person treats me is not a reflection of me, but a reflection of who they are. I used to think that there was something wrong with me or that I was doing something wrong. However, as I looked inside and analyzed my behaviors, I realized that I wasn't doing anything wrong. This was not a reflection of the Navy either. It was actually a reflection of those individuals' insecurities and poor skill sets. My experience, in fact, played a big part in shaping my leadership style. I learned that leadership is not about the position or the power. Leadership comes with a responsibility to not only do the job that you are expected to do, but also a responsibility to the people that you are leading and serving. As a leader, you are responsible for creating a culture in which people will learn, grow, and succeed in efficiently completing the tasks set before them. Leadership is about service. Over the years, I strived to be a servant leader: a leader that empowers others to reach their full potential.

Of the many lessons learned, I feel the most important lesson I learned from my experience is how to be responsive instead of reactive. Before joining the military, I reacted to everything that was said or done to me. The result of reacting first seemed to always turn ugly because there was little to no thought involved. Initially, I reacted to the way that I was being treated at my Command by picking up habits that were detrimental to my health and my way of life. I soon learned that reacting was destructive. As I grew, I switched from reacting to responding. A response required me to think things through and consider the consequences of my actions. I learned that responding proved to be a more productive and positive way to handle things. As I began to respond to people and situations instead of reacting, I felt better. It was less stressful. Responding gave me the strength needed to remain calm in situations where I was being mistreated. I have learned to maintain my composure and to respond in a way that is appropriate, professional, and productive.

Tap into the Resources

With strength and courage, I was not only able to live through that traumatic experience, but I asked for help in dealing with my emotions surrounding my experience. I realized that I was not going to make it if I remained in solitude. So, one day, I made the decision to live my dreams instead of my fears. Thus, beginning my ongoing healing process at a VA Medical Center. The VA Medical Center provides the services necessary to meet my unique needs. Reaching out to the VA Medical Center for care put me in a position that made me comfortable to begin sharing pieces of my military story with my family. As I began sharing my truth with my family, I felt a release and I felt my strength returning. The support of my family helped me to stay focused on my treatment and to accept my new normal.

Another vital resource in my journey to wellness was the Disabled American Veterans (DAV). I became a Life Member of the DAV, an organization that provides free services to assist Veterans in their transition from military to civilian life. The camaraderie helped me to see that I was not alone in what I'd experienced. I learned that there are other Veterans, both men and women, who share a story like mine. That truth gave me the courage to open up. The DAV also helped me get into a retraining program called Vocational Rehabilitation. Under Vocational Rehabilitation, I obtained both my bachelor's and master's degrees, enabling me to begin my new career path as an educator. My new career was rewarding. Over my 17-year career, I taught all grade levels and all subject areas in addition to teaching four classes as an adjunct professor. I have positively impacted many lives through teaching, mentoring, coaching, and volunteering. I continue to impact lives daily as I advocate for Veterans through my continued volunteer work with the Disabled American Veterans. In fact, in 2016, I became DAV's first female Commander for the state of North Carolina.

I am forever grateful for the Veterans Administration, the Disabled American Veterans, and my loving family. Yes, my experience was challenging, but it did not break me. I am still standing strong. No, I did not get here overnight, and this journey is a continuous one, but at no point did I give up on myself. Ultimately, my experience shifted my perspective on life. I now focus only on the positive in every situation. I made the decision to live by taking advantage of the resources available to me. Help is available to us, but we must conjure the courage to live and not merely exist, post military. Living my experience, working through my feelings surrounding my experience, and growing from my experience is the reason I stand today as a living testimony that we are not our circumstances. We can pick ourselves up and move past unfortunate circumstances with courage and the right resources.

A TESTING OF FAITH: LESSONS IN THE WILDERNESS

☆ ☆ ☆ ☆ ☆

LESLIE M. DILLARD

It was December 2013 and I had just settled into my position at the Pentagon on the Army Staff as the Branch Chief for Force Protection in the Army G8 when I received a phone call. As she began to read me my rights, I laughed as I thought it was some sort of joke. I asked the person on the other end of the line to stop playing. She emphatically told me this was not a joke and asked if I understood my rights. Taken aback, I asked, "Who is this again?" "This is the Inspector General's (IG) office, US Army Europe." It was then that I realized the severity of what she was saying, and I sat straight up in my chair. I told her I understood my rights and asked what next. After she explained the IG process, I thanked her and hung up. I sat at my desk staring at the phone trying to get my head wrapped around what had just happened. My mind was racing, "You have got to be kidding me!" Anger, hurt, shock, and disbelief filled my heart and head. After several minutes, I gathered myself and asked God, "Why me?" Not even waiting for His answer, I called my lawyer.

"It has taken me over 30 years to build my reputation and these Soldiers who have no clue of what integrity is are intent on taking me down! I have done nothing but provide them opportunities to excel yet they choose to be deceitful, taking conversations and situations out of context. Who does that?"

That was the start of the initial conversation with my lawyer as I was facing two IG investigations after leaving command. I survived a 15-6 prior to leaving command, but the IG investigations didn't follow suit. It didn't seem like it at the time, but what I didn't realize was God was working things out in my favor.

In the Beginning

As a young child, I watched my father put on his uniform and go to work. As a career Army man, my father had several pairs of boots and I always found my feet in them clunking around the house. They were always spit-shined before I got into them and scuffed by the time Dad came home. But, there was something inside of me that knew that I would pursue a life in the military. I even had an imaginary friend named Sergeant Major. We were inseparable and this relationship, such as it was, defined my first experience with a battle buddy. My grandmother tells the story that one day, when I was four years old, Sergeant Major and I were with my her at the laundromat when a little girl came in and sat down beside me. I quickly stood and told the little girl that she could not sit there, she was sitting on Sergeant Major. She promptly jumped up and apologized to Sergeant Major and moved down one seat! My grandmother smiled and said, "Now, if that's not a command presence and influence, I don't know what is." So, it began. On December 28, 1983, at the age of 18, I joined the Army and shipped off to Fort Jackson, SC. I was assigned to B-4-1 on Tank Hill, totally buying into the motto: "Victory Starts Here!" I excelled as a Soldier and knew I had found my niche in life, my purpose if you will, or so I thought.

The Fiery Furnace—Trials and Tribulations

"My brethren, count it all joy when you fall into various trials, knowing that the testing of your faith produces patience" (James 1:2-3, NKJV).

I would never have imagined that some 40 years after that encounter in the laundromat, I would be facing the biggest trial of my professional life. You could never have told me that after 30 plus years of exceptional service, two Soldiers being disciplined for poor performance would lead to: accusations of sexual harassment, creating a hostile environment, the mentorship of a Soldier being taken out of context and twisted into an accusation of involvement in an inappropriate relationship with a subordinate, and reprisal against a whistle blower. While the 15-6 investigation cleared me, the IG complaint did not. Those that have looked at this case don't understand how it got to the point that I was pulled off the O6 Colonel promotion list, effectively ending my dream of becoming a General Officer in the United States Army. I asked myself, how did I get here and how did my life go so horribly wrong? How could Soldiers that were eventually caught up in a court-martial impact the plans I had for my life? What about my good name? How will my Soldiers ever look at me the same? This was the road I would have to travel for four years as I fought to right an injustice that had been done to me and several of my staff, all the while continuing to do the job expected of me and displaying unshakable faith in the system I defended for more than 30 years.

What precipitated this laundry list of accusations you ask? Disgruntled Soldiers, pure and simple. I have always prided myself on being a person that will work with you. I always see the good in a person and try not to assume the worst. That's how I was raised as a Soldier. My very first NCO, 1SG (R) Annie Mickle, would always say, "Leslie, you must always take care of your Troops!" And that's exactly how I approached any situation—what is best for the Soldiers getting the mission done? But when there is a negative response or no improvement, consultation with the Soldier's rater and formal counseling were my tools of choice. For 30-plus years, Soldiers took the counseling, made the suggested or advised adjustments, and kept it moving. That was not the case here.

And before long, I was confronted with the aforementioned complaints. I didn't even see it coming!

Someone's Always Watching, but so is God

There is nothing more difficult than having to keep a positive attitude when I know there are co-workers that have a disdain for me. Their stated goal—destroy me. Regardless of what I was dealing with, I still had to get up every morning and show up, do the job, and complete the mission. As a Senior Leader, there was no other option. I could not give up on the Soldiers that depended on me. I still had to work with my accusers to accomplish the mission. I continued to smile and enjoy the small victories of Command. Over the four years that these investigations were conducted, I did not waiver in doing my job. I continued to excel and receive exceptional evaluations. As my case moved through the system, I continued to be selected for key positions and I was confident that I would be exonerated. I had no idea how many people were watching to see how I would handle the pressure of being under such scrutiny.

I must admit that while outwardly I displayed confidence and peace, inwardly I was hurt, angry, discouraged, and I had lost confidence in who I was as a leader. I asked God on several occasions, "Why me? Will the reputation that I have built over 30 years be destroyed by a couple of Soldiers?" As an African American female and a Senior Leader in the US

Army, I quickly realized that my life is analyzed and scrutinized beyond what I thought was humanly possible. Not everyone is cheering for you or watching in awe at how you accomplish the impossible. On the contrary, some are watching to find a weakness that they can exploit. I was blessed to be an influential leader and I was concerned that the investigation would negatively impact the many men, women, and children I mentored at church, in the community, and across the Army. It wasn't long before God answered with a Scripture from Isaiah 54:4a: "Do not fear, for you will not be ashamed; Neither be disgraced, for you will not be put to shame" (NKJV). God kept me covered and my name was never disgraced. However, what I discovered in that whole ordeal was that my plans weren't God's plans.

"For I Know the Plans I Have for You..." *(Jeremiah 29:11)*

As I look back over these past five years, I can see God's handprints all over my life. My constant nagging to the Father about "Why me?" came into focus when He said, "Why not you? Leslie, have you ever stopped to think that I have a greater call on your life than the US Army?" I was dumbfounded. Had I missed something God was trying to convey to me all this time? Was I truly headed down the wrong path? What I reluctantly discovered was that my season was coming to an end with the Army. The life I had known for more than 30 years was ending by divine design. My tour at the Pentagon came to an end when Human Resources Command (HRC) reassigned me to Fort Leonard Wood, Missouri. The conversation with the Branch Manager was brief as I accepted the assignment. I asked God if this was going to be my wilderness experience. Sometimes we equate the wilderness with negative experiences in our lives, but it can actually be a positive thing that propels us into our destiny.

In August 2015, with two investigations still hanging over my head and loaded down like *The Beverly Hillbillies*, I packed up my truck and moved to Fort Leonard Wood, Missouri. I didn't understand at the time that what was about to transpire over the next two years would be a personal and professional transformation and transition that only God Himself could have orchestrated.

"I am the Bishop of Your Soul"– A Pastor That Doesn't Give Up

"For you were like sheep going astray, but have now returned to the Shepherd and Overseer of your souls" (1 Peter 2:25, NKJV).

There is nothing like a pastor who will obey God and push you even when you don't want to be pushed. Standing about five feet tall, you wouldn't think she could push anything, but Pastor Marshall commands the room from the moment she walks in. We bonded immediately and then it happened, the conversation that started a chain of events that set me on the course to fulfilling my purpose.

Pastor Marshall: "Leslie, you need to join the Minister's Training Program, we start in January."

Me: "Uhhh, I teach I don't preach, Pastor."

I'm thinking, "She doesn't know me," as I turn and head for the door. "I'm definitely in the wrong church. This ain't the one for me. Minister's Training? She's got to be kidding!"

Pastor Marshall: "When you stop running, come back and see me."

I stopped dead in my tracks. Throughout this whole ordeal, I had been asking God the proverbial "What the what?" By this time, one investigation process had been going for three years, the other for two, and God had moved me to the middle of nowhere! In my spirit, I knew she was right. I had no doubt that she had already heard from God and He had me right where He wanted me.

God has a way of showing us our faults. You know that they exist, and you think you have done everything to fix them, but only God can bring you face to face with your shortcomings in a way that will knock the wind out of you. The answer to the "Why me?" was that I had been disobedient and prideful, but most importantly, I had replaced God with the Army. He had been trying to get my attention for a while, but I didn't listen. I didn't want to listen. So, He did what He does—change the circumstances so I would listen! Fort Leonard Wood became my training ground for my next mission—ministry, and Pastor Susan Marshall was the Drill Sergeant. God was truly intentional in bringing me to Fort Leonard Wood. I would not have gotten what I needed anywhere else.

Lessons Learned– Growth in the Midst of the Storm

I took away many lessons from my experience:

1. Pride. Pride, pure and simple. There is truth to the Scripture that pride comes before a fall (Proverbs 16:18). My thinking was flawed, and God used the situation to change my perspective. The Army had become my god. I had not allowed humility to be properly positioned in my life. God removed the idol and my heart began to bow.

2. Documentation. As the Senior Leader, I did not effectively document my concerns and conversations as I interacted with those Soldiers. Don't rely solely on others, document expectations and shortcomings of Soldiers for yourself.

3. Communication. Generational differences in our formation caused communication conflicts. Baby Boomers and Gen Xers trying to work with millennials is not a bad thing, but the differences in how we

communicate created problems with perception and understanding. I was not proactive in addressing the generational gap and the unit suffered as a result.

It's hard to admit that I made mistakes and could have done a better job overall. But, a leader committed to growth can admit their mistakes, and that is the type of leader I am. My greatest lesson was understanding that God uses every opportunity to get me where He needs me to be.

It Was Necessary

My wilderness experience turned out to be the best thing that ever happened to me. While the going through was difficult (yes, downright painful), I have come out as gold. Well, almost. I still have lots of growing to do, but I can relate to Job 23:10 that says, "But he knows the way that I take; When he has tested me, I shall come forth as gold" (NKJV). While the outcome was not what I wanted, it was what God wanted. God is blessing me exceedingly abundantly above all that I could ask or think. Because of His grace, I weathered the storm. Because of His purpose, I came out of the wilderness and I am stronger and more attuned to what He is requiring of me. I am a warrior. I will always be a warrior. I am a warrior for the kingdom of God. This journey is not about me or attaining rank. I am a vessel to be used for His purpose. My faith was tested and my purpose was revealed. It was all necessary!

SHIFT YOUR FOCUS

☆ ☆ ☆ ☆ ☆

EDWINA O. FREEMAN

Don't focus on your setback,
focus on your comeback.

The Setback

Have you experienced a time in your life when things were going quite well and suddenly you received some news that changed everything? If so, then you are not alone. I have been there and done that. Things were going quite well in my life upon my arrival at Howard Air Force Base in December 1992. A year before the arrival, my now ex-husband departed on a one-year unaccompanied remote tour to Korea. I stayed behind at Seymour Johnson Air Force Base, North Carolina, with our oldest son who was two years old. I was also three months pregnant with our youngest son. During my ex-husband's tour, he got promoted to Technical Sergeant, and I moved up to Staff Sergeant. So, having the family back together in Panama along with the promotions was an incredibly exciting time for us. However, a few months after our arrival in Panama, I became ill. Despite numerous tests, my doctors were unable to make a firm diagnosis. In September 1993, I was referred to Brooke Army Medical Center (BAMC) in San Antonio, Texas, to undergo a medical evaluation. The diagnosis of BAMC was fibromyalgia, a chronic disorder characterized by a multitude of symptoms including: widespread musculoskeletal pain accompanied by fatigue, insomnia, nerve pain, morning stiffness, headaches, and depression. Another common characteristic is cognitive difficulties also known as "fibro fog" which reduces a person's attention span and their ability to focus on mental tasks. These symptoms affected me physically, mentally, emotionally, socially, and spiritually.

A few years went by and I became overwhelmed and frustrated trying to raise a family, maintain a successful military career, and cope with a disorder that adversely impacted my personal and professional life. At one point, my musculoskeletal issues worsened to the degree that I was referred to a Medical Evaluation Board to determine if I was medically fit for continued service. The Board decided to allow me to remain on active duty. But, my issues did not stop there. I had other problems, and they were just as stressful as fibromyalgia. Both of my sons received a diagnosis of Attention Deficit Hyperactivity Disorder (ADHD), and marital issues began to set in. With no cure for fibromyalgia, I faced the daunting challenge of finding effective ways to manage and live with this disorder. I also had to find a way to keep my marriage intact and help my sons get through their problems. So, the search was on, and it took me down a path that would change my life forever.

The Shift

One thing I was sure of since middle school was that I was destined for the military. To prepare for the military, I served three years in Air Force Junior ROTC while in high school and came on active duty immediately after graduation. My goal was to retire from the Air Force, and that goal never changed. Even after being diagnosed with fibromyalgia and the issues that came along with it, I could not let that cause me to fall short of my goal. I was determined to find a way to fight and win. Initially, my approach was ineffective because I was out of balance. To make up for the times when I wasn't feeling well (which was quite often), I would go to work early, stay late, go in on weekends, and take work home in order not to fall behind. By any means necessary I had to remain on top of my game. In doing so, I exerted so much time and energy into trying to stay on top that when it came to my family, and more importantly God, I was exhausted. I managed to squeeze in some time for my family but spending time with God was something I did when and if I felt up to it.

Eventually, things reached a point where I realized that I could not continue on that path. In addition to fibromyalgia, I faced more life-changing situations. After relocating from San Antonio, Texas, to Hurlburt Field, Florida, in the year 2000, my husband and I separated, and he later filed for divorce. Subsequently, the court granted him custody of our youngest son which was our mutual decision. The stress from going through the divorce caused my condition to worsen both physically and mentally. I lost a lot of weight, slipped into an intense depression, and had to seek psychiatric treatment. My sons struggled in school and at home because of issues relating to ADHD and the divorce. I was in the fight of my life. If I was going to succeed in life, take care of my sons, and remain in good standing in the Air Force, I had to find another way to win. That is when I gave my life to God and asked Him to help me and to place me on the right path. That path led me to New Life Deliverance Temple Church. That was where I met Bishop Mark Williams and Apostle Brenda Williams who became the most dynamic influences in my life. Under their ministry, not only did I study and learn to comprehend Bible Scriptures, but I also learned how to make those Scriptures applicable so that they would work for my good in every situation.

One particular Scripture transformed my way of thinking and marked a significant shift in my spiritual, personal, and professional life. The Bible says in Romans 8:28 (The Amplified Version), "And we know [with great confidence] that God [who is deeply concerned about us] causes all things to work together [as a plan] for good for those who love God, to those who are called according to His plan and purpose."

A profound revelation came to me as I studied this Scripture and associated it with everything taking place in my life. I now realized that God cared about me and everything happening to me. None of my issues caught God by surprise. He knew these things were going to happen, and He wanted to help me; but, I had to surrender and turn matters over to Him. In fact, all of it was part of His plan and purpose for me. Finally, it resonated with me that neither fibromyalgia nor divorce could stop me from winning in life and in my career.

By 2002, two years after I went through one of the most traumatic times in my life, I was promoted to Master Sergeant, and I retrained into a new career field after 15 years in my previous field. As a Senior Noncommissioned Officer (SNCO), increased levels of responsibility and higher expectations came with that status. Being in a new job at the apprentice level did not exempt me from being held to high standards. The promotion was part of God's plan, so I continued seeking and relying on Him for guidance and wisdom. With God directing my steps, I was prepared to take on the challenges that came my way. He showed Himself strong and mighty on my behalf. Between 2003 and 2004, I completed two associate's degrees and I received the Air Force Meritorious Service Medal. Also, during this time, the Air Force Physical Training (PT) Program became more stringent. Members were now required to do push-ups and sit-ups in addition to the one and a half mile run. I refused to allow the thought of failing a PT test as an SNCO to enter my mind. Even with physical limitations, I never sought medical waivers to be exempted from testing. I desired to take the PT test and pass with a respectable score. Without fail, I always had at least one co-worker who was super gung-ho when it came to PT. They are the ones I connected with to maintain my motivation. Once more, because my career success was part of God's plan, I never failed a PT test. I scored well above average for my age group and gender. In 2005, I received another Air Force Meritorious Service Medal and my third associate's degree while assigned to Kunsan Air Base, Korea. I was not just merely succeeding in my career, God caused me to thrive.

Culminating my Air Force career, my final assignment was at Headquarters Air Force Special Operations Command (AFSOC), Hurlburt Field, Florida, in August 2005. I was requested by name to serve as the Engineering and Installation Program Manager for the Command. I was elated about being selected because another goal of mine was to work at the Major Command level before I retired. Once again, I found myself in a winning position. This assignment was the most exciting and rewarding assignment of my career. Promotion to Senior Master Sergeant was a real possibility. My supervisor, Functional Manager, and Deputy Director groomed me for it. However, I heard God say it was time for me to retire and I obeyed Him. So, in March 2007, I transitioned from military to civilian life with my third Air Force Meritorious Service Medal in five years and three SNCO of the Quarter awards from my tenure at AFSOC. More importantly, it was through this assignment that God reaffirmed that I remain at New Life Deliverance Temple Church under Bishop and Apostle Williams.

Several months before my selection, the assignments section at the Air Force Personnel Center advised that the assignment would not be available by the time my tour of duty in Korea came to an end. I vividly recall speaking with Apostle Williams about returning to Hurlburt Field, and she boldly declared that I was coming back to Florida. My heart's desire was to return to Florida and reunite with my church family at New Life. So, when I received notification about the assignment, my thoughts immediately went back to Romans 8:28. I knew it was not a coincidence that the job became available at the end of my tour in Korea. It was part of God's plan and purpose that I go back to Florida. I went through some immensely trying experiences during my career, but I would not trade them for anything. God turned around the adverse situations in my life and caused them to work together for my good.

The Comeback

Fast forward to 2018, 26 years after my story began and 11 years after retirement from the Air Force, and things are far from perfect. But, I am living a maximized life and I have an abundance of joy, peace, and gratitude. I focus on those things. I am still reaping the benefits from the experiences and lessons learned during the time of my setback and shift.

When challenges come my way, I reflect upon those times, and I see how God delivered me with His mighty hand. And if He did it before, He can do it again. Once I was broken, but God healed me and made me whole. So, I don't wallow in discouragement because God has a proven and consistent track record of bringing me out of every situation. Whatever you are dealing with right now, I encourage you to allow God to direct it from here. I admit you will experience some turbulence, but with God as your pilot, you will encounter a smooth landing.

Dear friend, God never intended for your setbacks to destroy you. He wants you to turn your setbacks over to Him so that He can use them to shift you and bless your life in ways you never imagined. Look at how setbacks positioned me to co-author a book and enabled me to share my story with you. What a comeback! God never ceases to amaze me with how He uses ordinary people like you and me to do extraordinary things. Suppose you shift your focus and begin to see your situation as an opportunity for God to use you to do incredible and unprecedented things that will bless people all around the world? Pause for a moment and imagine what your comeback will be like if you decide to shift. After you are done imagining, I encourage you to press full speed ahead and make the shift. I can assure you that it is one of the best decisions you will ever make.

BATTLE SCARS ON MY JOURNEY TO GREATER

☆ ☆ ☆ ☆ ☆

LATISHA D. WILSON

"'The latter glory of this house will be greater
than the former,' says the Lord of hosts, 'and in this
place I shall give [the ultimate] peace and prosperity,'
declares the Lord of hosts."

—*Haggai 2:9 (AMP)*

The Former Things

As female Soldiers, Veterans and spouses, we must be able to embrace who we are at all echelons of our lives. Each of us has a story that was erected long before we donned the uniform or loved someone who served. I wish that our stories were filled with only happiness, roses, and sunshine but that simply isn't the case. The fact is that many of our stories are laced with heartache, pain, and tragedy.

My story began when I was born to a 15-year-old unwed mother. She was my shero who loved me unconditionally. She was my mother, my friend, and my provider. She had a smile that lit up the world. And next to my grandmother, my other shero, she was the best cook I had ever known. Tragically on November 3, 1990, at the age of 10 years old, I witnessed my mother and baby sister die in a house fire. It was at that traumatic moment in my life that I believe my purpose was realized. Instead of crying and falling apart, I followed the lead of my grandmother and began to comfort and serve others, specifically my three-year-old baby brother.

That may seem like a young age to accept that I had a calling on my life to help others, but I did. I knew I was destined to encourage, inspire, and help others overcome situations, relationships, and behaviors that were unproductive and detrimental. Most of all, I wanted to be the best that I could be and excel at every task so that I would never disappoint my mother. She always let me know that I was special and destined for greatness, and I believed her with my whole heart. Yet, living out my life's purpose would not come without mistakes.

Fast forward three years. I'm 13 years old, in the eighth grade at Altheimer-Sherrill High School, and I'm thriving. I was a basketball star, a cheerleader, in the school band, singing in both my school and church choirs, and an honor roll student. And oh yeah, did I mention I was pregnant and a Christian? I know, wow, pregnant at 13! Most people, once they found out, dismissed all my accomplishments. They refused to acknowledge any unique qualities or attributes that made me, me. Have you ever dealt with the dilemma of being defined by a single act, mistake, or role?

I was more than just an unwed teenage mother. To my heavenly Father, my son, my grandparents, my true friends, and most of my family I was still a child of God. I was still a good hard-working student, a great athlete like my mom, and a great person with a purpose and a future. Having my son, losing my mom, and many other situations in my life left me with visible and invisible scars. Scars that represent my ability to overcome. Scars that represent strength. As women, we must learn to see the beauty in our scars. They are the roadmap to our true essence and maturity.

We can walk in our truth and beauty without dwelling on the heartaches of our tribulations. The key is to understand that despite what we go through, as children of God, we will always be victorious in the end. Know that it's okay to acknowledge our vulnerabilities while also embracing our strength. Sisters, it is my desire to take you on a journey that entails all of who I am, because of whose I am. I want you to realize through reading about my journey, as you reflect upon your own, that you are an overcomer, a conqueror, and a victor. You deserve to shine because you are no ordinary woman. You are a child of the King. You are a queen!

My Journey

If you are in the midst of a hardship and hurting, you may feel you have no way out. But, I am here to tell you to keep hope alive. Help is just a prayer away. I am so thankful that my bad choices didn't cancel God's purpose for my life. I'm thankful that His grace and mercy were sufficient for my journey because things could have been so much worse.

In September 1997, my senior year in high school, I joined the US Army Reserves. Yes, life was challenging, but I was still blessed and this was something I wanted to do. Shortly after graduating as salutatorian of my class in June 1998, I left for my Basic Training and Advanced Individual Training (AIT). I'll be honest, it was tough and there were times I wanted to quit. But, I remembered that my purpose was bigger than me, so I stuck it out and I am grateful I did.

In 2001, I decided to make the transition from Reserves to full-time active duty status. During that time, I also married the love of my life. Those were two life-changing decisions I will never regret. Soon after leaving for training in Fort Lee, Va., one of the worst days in our nation's history occurred, September 11, 2001. I was scared and filled with doubt about my decision to go active duty. But by faith, I remained steadfast and committed to my purpose to serve and be an example of courage and strength to my family, friends, and others God placed in my path. God had a mission for me and I had to truly trust Him.

I wish I could say this tragic event was the only dark moment in my career, but it was not. Being on active duty was a complete change for me. Coming from a small town, I was unprepared to face the harsh reality that racism and sexism existed. I quickly learned that not every leader was equipped to lead. Now listen, these things were not constant occurrences, but they happened more than they should have. No one should have to deal with discrimination, and as women we must speak out against it for ourselves and others.

As a black female in a predominantly white male organization, I felt I had to fight for every promotion and recognition I received over the course of my military career. But, that just reminded me of who I was long before I entered the Army. I was a leader, destined to win, and I was a child of God. I was able to see my challenges as opportunities to excel and overcome. God used those trials to show me that no weapon formed against me shall prosper, and every tongue which rises against me in judgment, He shall condemn. This was and is my heritage as His servant (Isaiah 54:17, NKJV). You see, it didn't matter how many times or ways Satan tried to stop my shine, I always came out brighter on the other side.

I fought for every promotion, from Sergeant (E5) to Sergeant First Class (E7). I had leaders who should have been mentoring me, but instead they were doing everything they could to keep me down. Nevertheless, I prevailed in the end. Not because I was perfect, but because God said each promotion was mine. Psalm 75:6-7 says, "For promotion comes cometh neither from the east, nor from the west, nor from the south. But God is the judge: he putteth down one, and setteth up another" (KJV).

I remember how the Battalion 1SG tried to block my promotion to Staff Sergeant (E6) by removing my name from the promotion board roster. He thought I would have to wait a full year after the Battalion returned from deployment before I could go to a promotion board. Since my unit was disbanding, I was not scheduled to deploy. Instead, I would leave Germany before they returned. The disdain was made worse when I wouldn't switch to a deploying unit in the place of a male counterpart who didn't want to deploy. Petty right! I didn't let this stop me. I kept a positive attitude.

One day, the Post Commander entered the dining facility and as usual I greeted him with respect, professionalism, and kindness. He asked me why I wasn't promoted. Not wanting to complain, I simply said, "I missed the board because of the deployment and won't get to attend before I leave Germany." He then said something to me that could have only come from God. He said, "Get ready, because in two weeks you will be going to the promotion board with me." The Post Commander held a promotion board just for me! Literally, I was the only one to go before the board that day.

I passed the board and my name was on the promotion list the following month, serving as reassurance that God remembers me when no one else will. When you have a purpose and promise on your life, the devil works overtime to deter you from receiving it. I know it was my positive mindset that allowed me to prosper in situations meant for my downfall. I know I am an agent of change operating in my God-given power. But even when you're strong in your belief in God, it still hurts when others intentionally try to ruin you and your career. No one wants to be overlooked or lied on simply because you are a woman, specifically a woman of color who isn't afraid to speak up, stand up, and shine.

I excelled, worked hard, went above and beyond what was expected, and *still* was not considered good enough or deserving of promotion. I refuse to accept mistreatment and will continue to fight for what is right. Despite the bad leaders I encountered, there were some really good ones that helped me develop as a Soldier and grow as a leader. I took to heart and truly lived the acronym "LDRSHIP" (Loyalty, Duty, Respect, Selfless Service, Honor, Integrity, and Personal Courage). I chose to be what right looked like.

My Latter

"Though your beginning was insignificant, Yet your end will greatly increase"—Job 8:7 (AMP).

I arrived at my new duty station in Arkansas on cloud nine. I was promotable and embarking on a new career field, Recruiting. My first few years were amazing. I was kicking butt and taking names. I was fast-tracking through the awards and was being recognized and rewarded for my hard work. I made it to the highest possible award, The Medallion, in half the time most others took. I was promoted to a leadership position as a Station Commander and was soon converted to a recruiter permanently. I was living the life and I knew I had God's favor. I got along great with my leadership and had their full trust and confidence. But, how many of you know that the sun can only shine for so long before a storm comes along? Not to hurt you, but to propel you to your next level of faith.

Shortly after I took over one of the largest stations in the Battalion, the leadership rotated out. This was nothing abnormal. The problem with this change was that the incoming leadership wasn't particularly fond of having a black female in this leadership position. At least that is what I concluded because after much success and no negative issues for four years prior, it was simply decided that I was no longer a good fit.

Soon, I was being looked at for my next promotion to Sergeant First Class (E7). The Battalion Sergeant Major (SGM) found ways to link me to every negative act that occurred, despite evidence that contradicted every accusation. I was plagued with flags on my personnel file while undergoing one investigation after another. The stress impacted every area of my life, not to mention I was facing infertility issues.

Despite the flag on my file, I had been selected for promotion and was on the promotion list! God had made a way yet again! No one could explain it. Of course, they tried to reverse it; but, the flag was removed when my promotion number came up and I was promoted. The leadership said it was an accident, but I know better. When God is promoting you, the devil isn't happy and he'll do everything he can to take you out (out of your mind, your peace, your health, and your position).

Even with the promotion, trouble still lingered. I was flagged again. This time it was meant to ruin my career, discredit my name, and have me put out of the military with nothing after 16 years of service. I was spontaneously put on orders to Korea and a code on my file barred me from being able to reenlist. I refused to accept that this was the latter my God had for me. And I am here to tell you that when you trust God and maintain your integrity, He will turn your mourning into dancing and give you beauty for your ashes. Because I was always on assignment from God and only on loan to the US Army for a season, God stepped in and I was rerouted to Fort Hood, Texas. It was there that He had me medically retired with full benefits. I didn't curse or slander those who were persecuting me, but God did have His vengeance.

What I went through didn't break me and the challenges you face won't break you. I just had to do the practical and let God do the providential. Nothing and no one can stop the promised life God has for me. So, I'm going to enjoy the journey knowing that it will propel me toward my greater. I chose not to become bitter, but better. I chose to thrive beyond my experiences. Those challenging times helped me to see that I wasn't pitiful, but a powerful woman of God destined for good success. Now, I am a testament that my "latter is truly greater" and the best is yet to come.

My Sisters, you are far more powerful than you realize. I can attest to the fact that God brought me through and He made it so that no one else could get His glory. He can and will do the same for you! God is going to do a work in you that will bless so many in your life and beyond. So, embrace your strength and your scars knowing that the story of your life is still being written and God will show you why He is the author and finisher of your faith. With Him you always WIN!!!

HEALING IS
A PROCESS

FINALLY FREE

☆ ☆ ☆ ☆ ☆

LEE ANN D. DAVIS

Keeping My Secret

Being mentally ill while serving my country was one of the most deceitful yet patriotic things I have ever accomplished. I never imagined those two words being used to describe me and my career. It doesn't sound very patriotic being deceitful, but that's how I survived as I struggled with a mental illness while on active duty. When I was first diagnosed with a mental illness, it was hard for me to accept it. I knew something was wrong with me. However, the fear of losing my career in the military due to the stigma of seeking mental health care made me deceive my Soldiers, my peers, my leadership, and most importantly, myself. I could not allow the words "mentally ill" to affect me since I received this diagnosis early in my career.

In my mind, I was doing the right thing by not getting help. The main reason I didn't reach out for help was that I did not want to be discharged and judged by others after I had been providing Soldiers leadership and guidance for over 20 years. What would the world say about another woman of color who had failed? What would my family and friends think of me? How would I ever work again? I would be a disappointment to my children. That fear was worse than the manic episodes of my bipolar disorder and depression that were first triggered by a traumatic military experience. That event, which I also kept a secret for fear of repercussions, only added to my erratic behavior.

Not realizing that the most important person in my life was staring back at me in the mirror, I always managed to isolate myself and not deal with my problems, as if they would just go away. At work, I acted as if I had no care in the world. I'm not saying that hiding my feelings made life easy for me, it didn't. One day I would feel on top of the world and the next I would feel like I wanted to erase myself from the world. The first time one of my leaders questioned my mental well-being, I was able to deceive him into believing I had mood swings because of my monthly feminine cycle. My body was always in constant pain, but I suffered through it after convincing myself that I deserved to be miserable because I was depressed all the time and did not appreciate life. I never really wanted to die, but my mind always played a game with me. I had someone in my head saying it would be ok to be in a coma for a while because that would give me a break from everyday life. The problem with that game is that I would never know just how many pills to take to put me in the coma yet not take my life.

Weekends were the worst. And, after an entire weekend of irrational thinking, I knew I needed to get help. But, I still talked myself out of letting someone into my world. I thought it was my alter ego helping me make it through some tough times in my military career. I internalized everything that happened to me. Some days, I would lose my self-confidence when I took my uniform off. On other days, the more I struggled, the more confidence I would gain in myself when I went to work.

The Secret is Almost Out

I advanced quickly in my career and responsibility was given to me. But unknowingly to my leadership, I was struggling to stay alive. By the time I became a Senior Noncommissioned Officer, I had mastered hiding my emotions. I was seeing a psychiatrist, but it still was not enough. I had two unsuccessful suicide attempts, but no one addressed those struggles with me so I kept quiet about it. I learned that the key to keeping my secret safe was changing duty stations. I found myself feeling ashamed and embarrassed when my Soldiers came to me for help with problems similar to mine and I did not encourage them to seek professional help. I needed them at work, and I was mission-driven. I would tell them the same idioms people would say to me, "Pray, stay strong, and if you don't want to get kicked out of the military and lose your clearance, you better keep your mouth shut. Now, let's get back to work!" No matter what the problem was, if their symptoms were like mine, I would not recommend going to see a mental health professional. I ensured that they also feared the stigma of mental illness as I did. I believe the reason that I did not get help was the perceived negative opinion that others would have about me being a leader in the military and making decisions with a mental illness.

I always wanted to stay busy and excel. I wanted to accomplish things I never could imagine, even if I had mental health challenges. I used my job as a crutch. I volunteered to deploy, I wanted to serve in every capacity that I could. I asked myself if I could be in a war environment and survive with a loaded weapon. The military mental health specialist had cleared me to deploy, so I assumed I could handle it. How did it become so easy to switch my emotions on and off? Why was it so natural for me? How was I such a different woman when I put on my uniform? I later realized I was having manic episodes due to my mental illness. I created two personalities, one for home that could be engulfed with the symptoms of my mental health issue and one for work that was strong and whose motto was: "Get it done or get out of the way." It wasn't a wise decision to deploy. However, God blessed me with a battle buddy that I would have entrusted with my life more than I would have entrusted myself.

As I recall, one time I did try to seek assistance. I was on medication, and I was mentally healthy for the first time in a very long time. Then, I had a significant event happen in my life and things were getting so difficult for me that I found myself in a mental health facility for days. They taught me how to practice self-care, which is learning to check in mentally with myself on a regular basis and identify harmful behaviors. But, I could not stop thinking about the adverse effects once my supervisor found out that I was suffering from a mental illness. At that time, I found comfort in knowing that I perfected my craft and I loved my job. Aside from my children, it was one of the things that kept me alive. Upon my return to work, my supervisor notified me that I was changing positions and being reassigned to a lighter duty. I felt incompetent, humiliated, and regretted getting help. Many of my Soldiers did not treat me the same after I was moved, and rumors skyrocketed. I knew the best thing for me was to change duty locations and try to salvage my career before other people in my field found out my secret.

I immediately decided that at my next duty station I was going to take my medication on time every day and get help up front, so everyone knew I had a standing appointment. Things were changing in my military career, and in the military. In less than a year, I relocated and tried to start over. My motivation stayed with me until the military began talking more about the "war on mental health." This topic skyrocketed and brought attention to some of the most tragic incidents within the military involving individuals who were mentally ill. I could not allow mental illness to take everything I had worked for in my military career like it did previously. I concentrated solely on my job.

Still Hiding

When I first became a Warrant Officer, it changed my life for the better. There were times that I would request leave, a pass, or just go TDY and get away so I could manage my depression or my uncontrollable emotions. I could step away for a while and regroup. The support from my leadership made minor situations a lot easier to handle, and there were few or no questions asked. I thought that the stigma did not affect Officers as much because in my experience they watched out for each other better than the enlisted did. I did know that it was much more challenging to take care of my mental health needs while I was enlisted. I had more people to answer to and I could not just say I had an appointment and leave. In the past when I would think about getting help, I would look around at the population of women I worked with and I knew it would cause me problems in the future. The military is actually small, and these were the faces of the women I knew I would see again. They were the faces of the women who would know my secret and later use it against me. I say this because I'd seen it happen before. However, as a Warrant Officer, I advanced in my career and I began to do things I enjoyed again. I met my best friend who later became my husband. His support was vital in my seeking assistance. After hiding my mental illness and struggling for so many years with no help, I was finally getting the care I needed, and I was at the height of my career. I could not believe the very thing

I had been running from, the stigma of seeking help from mental health services, was now keeping me alive.

That feeling of contentment all came crashing down when a doctor changed my medication. I remember going to work one morning feeling extremely tired and depressed. I sat at my desk for hours as the time moved, but I sat still. My emotions were going up and down. I began to feel anxious and overwhelmed. Before noon, I was in the refuge of my car crying, faced with the reality that I was finally done hiding. It was not a day that I felt like I could function as my alter ego and get away with it. Where was she hiding? Why wouldn't she come and save me?

After so many years of perfecting my alter ego and hiding my illness from others, I can honestly say that I did not know who I was. I left work, went home, sat on the edge of my bed, and grabbed a bottle of pills. As I began to take them—one, two, three, four… I thought about the unfinished tasks that I had left at work. I reached for my boots, still thinking about the mission first. But, the thought of just escaping for a while took over. I just needed a rest. So, I took more pills. I had vivid hallucinations that people were telling me to give up. As I sat on the bed and struggled to get up, I could not will my legs to move. As I fell back on my bed, I remembered the last time I said to someone, "I thought about going to see a psychiatrist," and that person told me that whatever I was going through I had better deal with it at home behind closed doors. If only they knew that putting myself into a coma was my way of dealing with it. By taking the pills that day, I thought that maybe I would finally be in the coma I had been striving to be in for so many years.

No More Secrets

It took me a while, but I FINALLY realized that I could not allow stigma, shame, guilt, embarrassment, or anything else to steal my life. I am not sure if I can give credit to the many trials of antidepressant combinations, mood stabilizers, electronic convulsive therapy, therapists, or just prayers for a mentally healthy life. However, I do think that God has been guiding me through this tornado so that I can help someone else. The only time that I feel a little peace is when I am with my family or volunteering in my community. When I was struggling with my emotions, the support from my family kept me grounded. Isolation for me meant life or death.

Being an advocate for mental illness has helped me tremendously. The thoughts and pictures of my unstable life without treatment are terrifying. Every day is a new day. I am no longer embarrassed to tell the world I have a mental illness. I have found that saying those words in front of other professional women has helped many of them expose their struggles to me. I've changed my motto to: "We are in this together" because we all have experienced hardships that may have left us questioning our mental instability.

Self-care is vital. What helped me was going to yoga, meditating, using positive self-affirmations, good music, dancing, and surrounding myself with supportive people. I now use my alter ego to ask myself how I am doing. I know we all tend to talk to ourselves sometimes, but this is the time it counts. Just changing the way I thought helped me improve my life. Some call that mindfulness. Today, I take my medication daily, my family is involved in reminding me to get refills, and they assist in monitoring my intake.

We all get sad, anxious, and at times frustrated, but if your emotions seem to be affecting your life negatively, you may need to seek professional help. If you are like me, maybe it's difficult for you to be transparent or maybe you are unsure of yourself when everyone around you thinks that you are on top of your game. Better yet, you may be great at hiding your true feelings and internalizing everything. You might even be experiencing chronic pain and not know why. Mental illness affects people in many ways. Start a mental health diary, track your emotions, and share them with your primary care manager. It took me years to realize how short life is and how much of it I allowed my mental illness to steal from me. It's time to accept that you may need to learn the importance of self-care even if you aren't suffering from a mental illness. It's FINALLY time to ignore the stigma, get help, and be in control of your happiness.

A JOURNEY TO HEALING

☆ ☆ ☆ ☆ ☆

DE'MEATRICE "DEE DEE" HODGES

The Long Road Home

You never know what you will face when you return home from war. There were many days I dreamt of seeing my daughter, friends, and family. When the day arrived and I finally boarded the plane home, I had many feelings racing through me. Then, the time came. We landed and got onto the bus to head to the same gym from which we left. Once there, I took a deep breath and stepped out of the door onto the pavement. My heartbeat was faster and louder than my own steps. I entered the gym, saw my daughter's beautiful big brown eyes and pig tails, and my heart melted. I was both nervous and scared. I must have been deep in thought because everything around me had become muted as I looked straight ahead, awaiting the next command. Suddenly I heard, "Dismissed," and fear took over. What would I say? How should I act? Those were questions that filled my mind. My daughter ran up to me and said, "Mommy, I missed you!" I could only cry as I reached down to pick her up. Those were the words I longed to hear for many months. She held on tightly. We cried together as she said, "I love you, Mommy, don't ever leave again." I cried even harder because I knew that was a promise I could not keep, so I remained silent.

After the celebration and time with friends and my church family, it was now just my daughter and me. At first, it was magical. I thought to myself, "It doesn't get any better than this." I laid my daughter next to me and watched as she went to sleep. As I slept, I could feel myself tossing and turning. I awoke in a puddle of sweat. Tears streamed down my face. My mind raced with images of death all around me. I saw kids jumping in front of vehicles desiring to be sacrificed for what they believed in. I couldn't imagine losing my daughter. I couldn't understand how a parent could sacrifice their child for a belief I considered to be a lie. I could no longer sleep; my heart was beating out of my chest. It was as if I was right there once again on the road in Iraq. All I could do was cry and mourn the loss of comrades who died during combat.

When my daughter opened her eyes, all I saw was love, but inside all I could feel was hurt and pain. I got up and dressed my daughter and myself. We got in the car and head-ed for her daycare. As I dropped her off, she cried and began to scream, "Don't leave me, Mommy!" The images of the children I saw on the roadside in Iraq flashed before me. I wanted to run, it was so overwhelming. I gathered myself, bottled up my emotions and spoke, "I'm not leaving you, I'm just going to work. I'll be back in a few hours." A calm came over her as she looked at me as I left. Although she was feeling more assured, I was torn. I got into my car and broke down.

I soon gathered myself and went to work. That seemed to be my routine for weeks. Dreams of death and war plagued my mind daily. I grew accustomed to masking the pain and sleepless nights. It reached the point where I became depressed and began to suffer from anxiety attacks. I no longer desired to spend time with my daughter or do the things she enjoyed doing. I became watchful, fearing that someone would try to hurt my daughter any time she was out of my sight. I had trouble sleeping at night and was tired during the day. All of this not only affected my work, but it began to impact my relationship with my daughter. I tried my best to hide what I was going through.

The Long Road to the Truth

As a leader, I know I should not have allowed myself to suffer in silence, but here I was—hiding the pain I faced because of my experiences during my deployment. One day while we were on leave (which should have been a joyous time), I fell into a deep depression. For the first few days, I tried to spend some time with my daughter by taking her to the movies and the park. It was good and we had a great time, but my nights were still full of nightmares and very little sleep. Many people think that it is easy to readjust after being in the military, but it is easier to don a mask than face your inner destruction. I felt like the things that took place during my deployment could have been prevented. Maybe there was *something* I could have done to change the outcome. I felt angry and frustrated because there was little I could do now to change what had happened.

My mind constantly returned to moments where I felt that I should have been the one that did not return home. I asked myself a thousand times, "Why?" That one question plagued me in such a way that I found myself writing strategies down on countless pieces of paper trying to figure out the answer. Not even the Purple Heart award I received, the loving looks from my daughter, nor the sweet kisses and hugs she gave me could block out the anguish, heartache, and self-blame I was feeling. Every time I closed my eyes, I relived the events over and over. The mental replay would not stop. I couldn't shake it no matter how hard I tried.

Nothing, not even going to church Sunday after Sunday, seemed to help. As a devout Christian, I was taught to trust and lean on God, to have faith, and to believe that healing would come. Yet, with all the Scriptures I knew to read, the constant praying, and even seeking prayer from others, I still only saw nothing but despair and darkness. My mind had become clouded with it. I continued to pray and talk to

God, desperate to find relief and freedom from all that I had seen and experienced. I remember talking to God and asking, "Why did you allow this to happen to me? Why can't I make it through?" Even though I asked, I heard nothing, which angered me even more. In my mind, I believed I was doing everything I could to get past my pain and overcome my obstacles. But, the truth was that I was not asking the right questions nor was I ready to hear or receive the answer.

I began to experience difficulties driving. Every time I got into the car I thought someone was following me. I avoided driving near things in the road to prevent being struck by an IED (Improvised Explosive Device). I thought to myself constantly, "Why is this happening to me? I am saved, strong minded, and a Soldier. I should be able to handle this." I felt like I was worthless, useless, and that the Army and my fellow Soldiers were better off without me because, in my mind, I was more of a liability than a help. I blamed not only myself for the things I was experiencing, but my leadership as well. It seemed that the more I looked for answers, the more I found myself placing the blame where it probably shouldn't have been. At one point, I wanted answers, at the next, I wanted revenge. In reality, I really just wanted peace.

This had been going on for a few weeks and I could no longer take care of my daughter by myself. I picked up the phone and asked her godparents to keep her for a while. I had become irritable and angry as well and snapped at her for no reason. She wanted to be with me every second of the day, but it became too much for me. I couldn't handle the amount of affection she gave me, I just needed space. I felt like a worthless mother. I didn't think I deserved her. I had looked forward to coming home so much, but now that I was home I couldn't even function properly. I thought that I was ruining her life and that maybe I was not the mother she deserved. A mother is supposed to be the provider, the comforter, and the strong one. But, here I was distraught, depressed, and somewhat lifeless. How could she ever look up to me again? Could I show her how to be a strong woman?

The Long Road to Healing

I began to lose weight from the stress and eventually lost my appetite all together. I suffered from migraines and I could not sleep. I was constantly on guard and looking over my shoulder. I stopped hanging out with friends and loved ones and tried to stay away from all that I had known and loved. I knew it was time to get some help; so, I started counseling while my daughter was away to make sure that I was not only an affective Soldier, but a productive, useful, and loving mother. The first thing the counselor asked me was, "Why are you here and what can I do to help you get to where you want to be?" I remember thinking to myself, "Why would you ask me these questions after I filled out all of the information that was required to see you in the first place? This is the exact reason why no one wants to get help." At first, I didn't really talk. Although I wanted the help, I was trained to be a Soldier first and feel later. It was embarrassing at one point. The counselor wanted me to be vulnerable and talk about my experiences during deployment, but how could I do that when I was a Soldier first?

I soon realized that the questions were not asked to upset me but to see where my mind was. I began to see a change in myself after a few visits, and then I started to understand that this was all for my good. I was able to bring my daughter home and continue to care for her as her mother who loved her unconditionally. The nightmares and anxiety did not completely stop, but I was able to use the tools and information I learned in counseling to overcome them.

I even began to hear God's voice clearly again. My prayers began to change. Instead of complaining to God, I thanked Him for allowing me to see another day that I had never seen before. Instead of asking the question "Why?" I began saying, "It's your will, God. Let it be done now and forever." My relationship with my daughter was better. I was the mother she deserved and needed. I now know that I was not alone; God had never left me. He was there all along. I just had to reach out to Him and those who had the knowledge to help me get to where I needed to be. What I went through was a life-changing adventure for me. Many may not understand the adventure part, but if you really think about it, our lives are all an adventure. We have ups and downs, but in the end we can overcome it all.

THE VISION TO SEE ME CLEARLY

☆ ☆ ☆ ☆ ☆

JANET WILLIAMS

Critical Thinking

"You're not as good as you think," was the statement I allowed to crumble my world. Those criticizing words came from a former supervisor that I'd hoped would teach me the keys of success to get to the next level in my career. I was a young Lieutenant in the United States Army, desperately in search of a mentor. Having a mentor was something preached at every Leader Professional Development session, and here I was thinking I had found "the one" only to be crushed by those words. I had been searching four years for a good mentor to provide guidance as I continued along my career path. I had such high hopes in this individual that I forgot where my help truly came from. And so began the drought...

It was a defining moment, an epiphany if you will, to un-expectedly embrace feelings of inadequacy from a critic. I wrestled with whether to use the critique as fuel for fire to propel me forward or to accept it as my reality. Over time, I began to question my abilities and why I even joined the military. Those words consumed my thinking. I allowed thoughts of past failures to resurface and I completely dismissed all successes I had accomplished thus far. Sound familiar? Have you or do you know someone that has gone down this path? We, too, can be our own worst critics. Going through such disappointment, I concluded that the thing that takes you down is the thing that can take you back up.

Blurred Vision

Vision is the ability to see beyond your current circumstances. In my youth, there was one question I could never get away from, "What do you want to be when you grow up?" The funny thing is, I still ask myself this question. I had ac-complished all that I wanted, or so I thought, until I hit a hard place when I finished my master's degree in transportation and logistics. Truthfully, I pushed through for years for career advancement. I had a mind to grow; therefore, I set goal after goal after goal. I became knowledgeable in many subjects, but my mind and body grew weary.

In 2006, I developed a habit of creating a motto for my-self to bring me into the new year, motivate me, and help me focus. From 2006 to 2007, my motto was "Fake It Until You Make It." From 2008 to 2010, it was "Make It Happen." From 2011 to 2013, I declared "It's Happening," and then I took my big break. Don't get me wrong, taking a break is good for rest, relaxation, and recovery. However, you must keep in mind that breaks are meant to be short-term and it is imperative to have a plan to get yourself back in the fight.

From 2014 to 2016, there was nothing, only silence. I had stopped dreaming, and for a moment in time, I died. Proverbs 29:18 discusses the importance of having a vision because without it the people perish. I had lost my vision and could not see clearly. I lost sight of my dreams. What did I *really* want to do now that I was "grown up"? I lost sight of myself and the value that I add to the team. It was not easy for me to get back into the game. I was in a dark place, mentally. I felt hopeless and constantly questioned my usefulness and self-worth. I felt I had lost control and was headed in a downward spiral. But, God has a funny way of getting you back on the right track with His clever life puzzles. I realize now that the following events in my life were God's way of setting me up for an escape and comeback from the darkness that had taken hold of me.

Refocused Vision

I was invited to a few events by a business network of entrepreneurs, Wealthy Sisters Network, which called for me to construct a vision board to start off my year. Stubbornly, I accepted the invitation and attended. Cynically, I compared this to declaring New Year's resolutions and believed that within a few months the hype would die down. Inspired by the cohesion of empowered women, I created my first board. It was incredibly difficult because I was not motivated, I could not see the future, and I had given up on myself. Nonetheless, I completed the board. A few weeks then a few months went by and I noticed that I was living my vision board. Slowly but surely, I came out of what I called a black pit. The next year came around and I created another vision board, though this time I decided to create a motto. I figured I would give the motto thing another try since it worked so well before. In 2017, my motto was "Push Until Something Happens (PUSH)." I'd heard that saying in many ways before, but it did not resonate with me until then. I focused on three areas with that board—life, family, and business. I can truly say that those three areas of my life were glowing with laser focused attention and great things happened that year.

One day I was talking with my mother and I asked her what kind of week she was going to have. She began to speak declarations and make decrees that hit me like a rush of wind. Suddenly, I imagined being in the eye of a tornado. She spoke her declarations with such conviction that I believed in that very moment what she said would come to pass. Excited about her week and motivated by her energy, I thought I'd give it a try as well. Hesitantly, I began to speak and before I realized it, I had spoken life into my week. At that moment,

I felt great and could not wait to see the manifestation. We ended our conversion with a prayer and she became my accountability partner. We set a time to conduct regular conference calls, invited others to join in, and week after week through the power of agreement, I became confident in my words and free in my mind. It does not matter where you are in life, you have the power to command your day and even your week. I challenge you to see yourself as great because your future self is counting on you!

The Formula

Sure, it is easier said than done. So how did I do it? Here's the formula:

1. Believe. The first step is to believe in yourself. Believing in yourself produces hope and sparks action. In other words, if you can believe, then it is possible.

2. Be Willing to Grow. Growth attracts success. The growth period is not always pretty and can be challenging to accept. Maintain an open mind and keep pushing.

3. Surround Yourself with Positive People. "Birds of a feather flock together" or simply put, you become like the people you hang around. This became so real to me that I began to carefully choose the people I wanted in my life. Not only that, I had to let go of

those that were no good to me or did not edify my life's purpose.

I won't tell you that implementing these steps was easy because it was not. It was a process. I remember attending a weekend retreat called Songwriting with Soldiers. My motivation was still up and down like a rollercoaster. One day I felt on top of the world and the next day I was drowning in self-doubt. I arrived at the retreat with a closed mind as if nothing could save me from shouting out a cry for help. To my surprise, I was amongst those that were lost and trying to find themselves as well. I was surrounded by Veterans and felt ashamed because my story did not even compare to the hurt and pain those women endured.

The retreat was full of events that revolved around self-help, something we often forget about because we're too busy being superwomen and taking care of everyone but ourselves. Self-help was extremely difficult for me, as I was trained to put on a face—one that is void of feelings. It was part of the military culture. I later discovered that I was hurting myself by not being openly expressive without shame or fear of putting my career in jeopardy. The highlight of that event was giving myself permission to let my guard down and be vulnerable enough to tell my story. After all, we're only human. Throughout the retreat, I developed some beautiful relationships with beautiful people that I can now call my sisters. By the end of that retreat, I became so comfortable that I agreed to co-write a song with a multi-talented singer and songwriter, Bonnie Bishop. Your environment is significant, so place yourself where you can be challenged to grow.

I soon learned to embrace that there is always room for improvement and that there will always be someone better than me. This was liberating for me. The pressure to be perfect was lifted. In addition to that, I learned to simply do my best and accept that my best may not be the best in someone else's eyes. In other words, there will always be critics. It may even be true that you are not the best fit for a certain position, nonetheless, always give it your best shot. Success is what you make of it. To some it is accomplishing goals, personal fulfillment, or simply being happy. Whatever it is, you have to define it for yourself. If I had to put a percentage on success, I'd say it is 10 percent verbal, 20 percent physical, and 70 percent mental.

Ladies, open your mouths and speak life into your situation. Consistency is key here, so make it a habit to say it, dream it, and live it. "Faith without works is dead" (James 2:20, NKJV) and as the old saying goes, "Actions speak louder than words." Be willing to put in some work, get your hands dirty, and BELIEVE (there's that word again) in yourself. The universe will comply with your desires. I am now a Troop Commander doing what I love, leading Soldiers. This very story, a product of my 2017 vision board, is one that I share with my Soldiers today. I use it as a tool to inspire others not to be afraid to orchestrate their lives. As Benjamin Franklin said, "If you fail to plan, you are planning to fail."

Who would have thought that constructing a personal vision board to guide my life's choices would work? Ironically, I am a visual person by nature, but never thought to create one for my life. I am grateful for the visionary behind the idea of creating a vision board. Today, I challenge you to take your life back; grab it by the loins and take it by force. Denounce self-doubt and be willing to take calculated risks. Do not allow life to pass you by. We were all created for a purpose, discover yours. In closing, I leave you with this to remember, "The sky is not the limit, your mind is."

A SHIP WITH NO ANCHOR

☆ ☆ ☆ ☆ ☆

TIFFANI K. PATTERSON

Finding My Identity

I was born the youngest of five. Both of my parents only had brothers, which makes it even more of an oddity that together they only had daughters. Many would dream a house full of girls would be filled with dolls, makeup, and all things girly, but we were raised different. While there were still dolls and some things girly, there were also bats, balls, bikes, hand me downs, and patched up holes in jeans that eventually were cut at the knees to make knee-knockers as my mother would call them. Being the youngest, I always had to fight for my spot in any conversation, my seat in the car, and my role in playing school, church, or any game that involved a hierarchy. That's where I earned my first stripes. Unlike my sisters who went to the same elementary, middle, and high school, I attended six different schools prior to landing at our high school, which allowed me to have my own identity. I was allowed the free-dom to build an identity without the Patterson stamp on it because no one knew of those who came before me.

Fast forward to high school where my sisters accomplished achievements that set them apart from others. One received a basketball scholarship to play at a then Division 1 college, another burnt up the track with records that might remain today. And, all were known for their skills in sports in addition to being all-around great students. Then came me, blazing through that school and burning down any chance of leaving the legacy that was almost predestined for me. I was different. Looking back on my actions, it was as if my goal in high school was to take everyone's great advice and do the opposite. And if a teacher were to even ask why I wasn't like my sisters, I almost worked even harder to get them to believe that there was no way we could be related. I'll admit, I wasn't the worst kid (there was no way that would happen with the strict parents I had at home), but I was an educator's pre-nightmare. All because I was trying to prove I was my own person. Fast forward to graduation where I made it across the stage. I still remember that day when my diploma was handed to me and the only thought in my head was, "What am I going to do tomorrow?" I was a ship with no anchor floating in the big sea of adulthood. I had made it, but what would adulthood make of me?

My first semester of college was a joke. Till this day I laugh at my lack of thought when picking my classes. "Piano… sounds good because my parents never got me lessons. English… I love to write… I will definitely pass this class. Criminal justice, sounds good. I might want to be a cop, I might not." It was a popular major then, so why not take it? After one semester (one in which I miserably failed criminal justice) and once the San Diego Zoo said I wasn't fit to hire because of a surgery I had as a teen, I went to my dad and told him I was going to join the Army, just like my two sisters. My dad, a 20-plus year Navy Master Chief, looked at me and asked what I thought about the Coast Guard. Till this day when I ask him why he told me not to join the Army, he says, "I don't know what it was, but there was something about you that made me know you would do better in the Coast Guard. I felt that the Army was not for you." Even though I never served a day in the Army, I know that my father was right. There is something about the Coast Guard that just fit me.

Setting Sail into Adulthood

To say that I loved the Coast Guard wouldn't be far from the truth, but it wouldn't be super close to it either. While serving, my feelings about the Coast Guard could go from like to love to hate depending on the day, but I was good at it. Even still, I was determined to create my own identity aside from what people thought I should be. Against my father's and other service member's advice, I chose to be a Boatswain's Mate (BM). By Coast Guard definition, a Boatswain's Mate is a master of seamanship. My father however served in the Navy and feared that my striking Boatswain's Mate meant that I was signing up to be the ship's janitor. I will admit being a Boatswain's Mate wasn't the most coveted rating (job) in the Coast Guard, but it was the rating that was showcased to get people to want to sign up in the first place. BM's had a reputation. Usually they were men, more specifically white men, who smoked excessively and drank so much coffee it stained their coffee mugs. They were the backbone of the ship, and it didn't matter whether you would admit to knowing it or not because they knew it. A major part of a BM's reputation was everything I wasn't nor wanted to be, but oddly enough, I still became one.

During my 9-year enlistment in the Coast Guard, I achieved many goals that I had never even set for myself. As a "boot" E-2, I operated the boom on the US Coast Guard Cutter (USCGC) Buttonwood (WLB-306), a 180-foot sea-going buoy tender, on various missions ranging from buoy tending to recovering debris from plane crashes and refueling the Farallon Islands. I was one of the first enlisted females on the ship and we worked vigorously to break down the barriers that came with the territory of being a female on a working ship. That's where I served with many important people in my career such as: Chief BMC Bradley (my first Chief), MK Sasse a.k.a. "Dee Mama" (the first female MK I ever met), and Officer Mrs. Cunningham (a black female who would go on to be the first African American female Captain in the United States Coast Guard). They shaped the success I achieved in both my Coast Guard career and my personal life.

I never went into the Coast Guard saying I wanted to be a BM, but Chief Bradley saw that I was a BM. When I submitted a chit to be placed on the storekeepers "A" school list, he took it, looked at it, and ripped it up. He knew that I picked SK because my father was one, and Chief also knew that I was not my father. He knew that being an SK would not fit me. I trusted his judgment and decided to strike Boatswain's Mate. Overall, he taught me not to follow in someone else's footsteps, but to be myself and make my own way.

MK Sasse was the leader of the pack for the enlisted females. She had enough service time under her belt to know that if she didn't guide the young new "boot" females, we were sure to drown; so, she took us under her wing and helped us to navigate the ways of the ship and stay on course. When we went astray, "Dee Mama" got us back on track. When I would complain about my job—having to change the lights in sea buoys and thinking that it was meaningless, she would remind me that a Sailor at sea has faith that there is a light to guide them home, and even though I see it as just a stupid light, that light was saving people's lives. She taught me to look at the bigger picture in situations and not to focus on the small stuff.

Lastly, Mrs. Cunningham was a former Honor Guard Officer whose uniform looked better than any Sailors on their best day. She was a model "Coastie." Despite us being stationed on a working ship, the dirtiest ship in the fleet, she stayed sharp. Mrs. Cunningham held herself to a high standard and didn't fold into the lax feel a working ship can have in comparison to an Honor Guard assignment. She was who she was despite the events happening around her. She was a goal-driven, dedicated person who worked hard to get where she was, and she was committed to working even harder to get where she was going. It was no surprise when it was announced that she had advanced to Captain (O-6). She taught me that goal setting is key and that what someone says no to can always be achieved another way.

My last four years in the Coast Guard were spent onboard the USCGC Hamilton (WHEC-715) homeported in San Diego, California. Upon reporting, I was a BM2. While stationed at USCG Group Charleston as a Master-at-Arms, I toyed with the decision to stay in or separate; but, advancing to E-5 heavily influenced my decision to reenlist. That and the fact that I could get stationed on a ship in my hometown. I would be offered two things I loved: access to the sea and being close to my family. The plan was to see if I could manage being in the military better with the consistent support of my family nearby. During my four years onboard, I once again achieved goals that I had never set for myself and took part in experiences that I couldn't have imagined. I became the first black and female Over-the-Horizon Boat Coxswain which involved me working on high-speed, open ocean drug interdictions and resulted in (at the time) one of the largest Pacific Fleet drug busts on a Coast Guard mission. I took part in many operational missions not limited to search and rescue on domestic plane crashes, enforcing fishing laws on the maritime boundary line, and guarding California's ports of entry during 9-11.

I advanced to E-6 and was in charge of 30-plus newly recruited "boots" and certain operational and administrative aspects of the ship. As a little girl, I couldn't have conceived or even dreamt of the missions I was a part of in the Coast Guard because they never existed in my world. Even still, I didn't see the Coast Guard as a career. I didn't see 20 years of service in my future, not active duty service to be exact. I wanted to teach. But, what I really wanted was my freedom back. I wanted to be in control of my own future and being in the Coast Guard didn't provide that for me.

My Path to Happiness

Deciding to separate from the Coast Guard wasn't an easy choice. I had a lot going for me. I was an E-6 with six years sea time under my belt, a lot of experience, and skills. None of which seemed to really matter because I wasn't happy. I felt restricted by the lack of freedom of choice. So, I ran the idea by my parents, partly because I needed them to provide me a place to stay as a college student and because I valued their advice on how or if separating would affect my future.

Despite having a well mapped out plan for my future, I was questioned many times by my shipmates about what I was going to do. How was I going to survive the "real world"? I was even told by one shipmate that I was dumb for throwing 9 years of service away. But what did they know? The military was a choice of mine, but it didn't make me who I was. It didn't define me as a person. I'll be honest, separating scared me, but I needed to pursue my childhood dream of being a teacher. I needed my life to be completely mine. I longed for the day I could make all decisions for myself, and I wanted to do that as soon as possible. So, even though I had signed up for the Reserves, I called my unit and informed them that I had changed my mind and I would no longer be a part of that either. I wanted to focus full-time on getting my bachelor's degree and my teaching credentials.

Looking back on everything I experienced and left behind, I can proudly say that being in the Coast Guard made me a better teacher. It gave me a unique outlook on life and the ability to offer a different perspective to my students. It made me appreciate life more and pushed me to work ambitiously toward my goals. Joining was one of the best decisions I made as a teenager, and separating was the best decision I made as an adult.

My time in service is proof that there is not a one size fits all method to life. Just because you do something well doesn't mean you were meant to spend the majority of your life doing it. Had I not separated, I would have never had the opportunity to be a mentor to many of my former students who are currently serving in various branches of the military or support the ones who are pursuing a higher education. I, like them, struggled with finding myself as an adult, and I owe it to the US Coast Guard for grooming me into who I am today. Now, I can proudly enjoy the freedom for which I served. And because of the influence of those who came before me, I have built an identity that interweaves being a Patterson and being a "Coastie."

FINDING STRENGTH FOR MY JOURNEY

☆ ☆ ☆ ☆ ☆

DEIA R. AUBREY

A Radical Decision

Growing up in Flint, Michigan, was not easy. I was the third of four children to a single mother. We were considered poor because we were on welfare. I never felt that way though. During my childhood, Flint was different. Today it is known as the dying city with the water crisis, but back then it was a bustling city of over 100,000 residents. It had its issues with crime and gangs, but there were several youth programs for inner city children to get involved in. Sports became my outlet at an early age. My earliest memories were at John F. Kennedy Elementary School. I was a smart student, usually making A's as a standard grade. At the same time, I still found my share of trouble. Whether it was a fight on the school grounds or mouthing off at the teacher, I received more than my fair share of detention and paddlings. To deter my troublesome behavior, I was introduced to all types of sports and I liked them all, including powder-puff football and basketball. Basketball became my love, and I was very good at it. I played varsity in ninth grade and was a starter. During those times, sports was a way out of the ghetto, so I thought I had found mine in basketball.

During my junior year, I was being heavily scouted by local Michigan universities, so it looked like my future was bright. I was a great student-athlete, and all looked well until my life took an unexpected turn. The scouts stopped calling and coming to watch, and my chances of getting out slipped away. My hopes and dreams of college did not go as planned, and I was now in my early twenties. I had already tried community college and I felt my life was at a standstill. So, I made a radical move and joined the Army. I wasn't foreign to the concept of the military because I had family members serving. An uncle in the Air Force, one of my older brothers was in the Army, and a cousin in the Marines. I had never planned to serve, but life in Flint seemed to be swallowing me up fast and I needed a quick getaway, so I enlisted.

My first duty station was Germany, and less than a year after being there I deployed to Desert Shield/Desert Storm. I was a signal Soldier during that time. Just before the war, the Signal Corps announced career changes were going to take place and Soldiers would be retrained to a more updated communications system. Some areas of the Army had already gone through the training, but not yet in Germany.

So, we were selected to deploy for the Gulf War because the Army needed Soldiers still operating under the old system. My days as a Signal Soldier were very happy. Although we trained in the field 10 months out of the year, I enjoyed Army life to the fullest. The job was fun, and the country I lived in was awesome. My brother and my uncle were also serving in Europe at the time, so I even had family to visit often. I met my husband and we married after dating for a couple of years. My Army life was shaping up to be a great decision. Until one day when my world was shaken to the core while stationed at Ft. Bragg, N.C. I received orders that I was being mandatorily reclassified from Signal to Engineer. I felt I had only just begun my career. I was only a Specialist at the time. What was going to happen? Here I was enjoying my career then suddenly I was being forced to do something I didn't want to do. I was devastated. I remember going into the latrine and crying uncontrollably for 20 minutes before I pulled myself together enough to call and share this awful news with my husband.

Mental Resilience for the Journey

There I was standing face to face with the 12th Sergeant Major of the Army (SMA) at Fort Wainwright, Alaska. The best and most famous SMA, in my opinion. "The One Arm Push Up SMA." I had crossed his path on many other occasions, but this one was special. It was my promotion ceremony to Sergeant First Class and he was there to pin on my rank! I was at my third duty station as an Engineer. My only hope was that this engineer thing had to get better. I was the only one in my organization that was selected to SFC. I remember controversial comments from some in my unit because I was new. I had just arrived in the spring, right when the promotion board convened. It was now fall and the board results were released. It was clear what type of leader I was, and there were those in the unit who decided they wouldn't be welcoming to a strong female leader. They were adamant about not making this a smooth experience. Not only were my Soldiers resistant, but my peers and Senior Leaders were too. What should have been excitement at that point in my career started the journey of mental toughness and resiliency on levels I had never thought or even imaged possible to get through.

Now considered a Senior Noncommissioned Officer (NCO), I had to uphold a new standard, walk a straighter path and a tighter line, and be almost perfect in some people's eyes—beginning with my First Sergeant (1SG). When he found out my sequence number came up and I would be pinning on my new rank, we had an interesting conversation. I'll just tell you that 1SG and I had history and it wasn't good history. I immediately became suspicious when he showed up to talk with me. I had learned that when dealing with him, real time prayer was needed. His words to me were, "You know you will never take over Earthmoving Platoon. There has never been a female in charge of the platoon, and we won't start with you." My response was, "Okay, 1SG, no problem. What job do you think you would have me continue to do?" His response was, "If you repeat this to anyone, I will call you a liar. I am going to keep you as a Squad Leader." At that point, I knew my journey as a Senior NCO was going to be even more challenging than the first seven years of experiences with my Engineer counterparts.

I did not let that conversation discourage me. And through conversations with higher leadership, I became the first female Platoon Sergeant of Earthmoving Platoon. There were personnel assigned to the platoon when I took over and there was only one other female besides myself. What a ride it was, too. We had some awesome construction projects, and it took us to some areas of Alaska that I never dreamed I'd get the opportunity to see. I was honing my craft as an Engineer. I was learning about geology and the different layers of the earth which advanced my knowledge of the career field. The strange thing about leading the platoon was that the males dislike for me as their leader caused them to become a very close-knit team, which externally reflected that Earthmoving Platoon had great camaraderie and teamwork. Isn't God good!

Fighting the Enemy Both In and Outside of the Wire

We were notified we would be deploying to Afghanistan. At the time, I was dual military and because of the deployment my husband would have to move without me. Additionally, I was nearing the end of my assigned duty as Platoon Sergeant. As the unit prepared for deployment, I suggested to my Command that we give one of my promotable Squad Leaders the opportunity to take on more responsibility in the role as the new Platoon Sergeant. His sequence number was one, so he would be promoted prior to the deployment. This made sense to me and would eliminate the dilemma of finding him another job once the unit deployed. The idea was heavily rejected and even perceived as me not wanting to deploy, which was not the case at all. If I had to deploy, I was ready to go; but, separating my family was causing me undue stress. The NCO was excited about taking the new position and all seemed to make sense in our minds. However, my chain of command had a different view. My new Commander took the opportunity to say what I guess was every negative comment that had been passed on to him from the previous Command.

I remember another Platoon Sergeant (male) that came forward and outright admitted that he did not think he could handle the mission downrange, but he was just given encouragement that everything would be alright once he got there. On the other hand, I was being treated like I had committed a horrible crime by asking not to be separated from my family.

The other family situation I was dealing with was that my mother was my dependent. She was on dialysis living in Alaska with me. The plan was to move her back to Flint and get her settled in an assisted living facility, but the dates did not coincide. The solution was that I would have to deploy a month after the main body to get her settled. I was met with much resistance when I put in this request. My Commander even threatened that he would chapter me for an improper family care plan. After explaining to him that he had in fact approved the family care plan I was attempting to implement, he had no choice but to let me take my mom to get settled.

I distinctly remember receiving a strange call from him a few days before I was to leave to take Mom back to Flint. He asked me if I was still on schedule to come or had I changed my mind. I remember responding that I didn't have a choice, and that after my mother was settled I would be in Afghanistan to do my job like everyone else. His only reply, "Oh."

I arrived at Kandahar Operating Base as scheduled and prepared to join the unit at the Forward Operating Base (FOB). I found it odd that when I was issued my M4 rifle, I was not given any ammunition. When I inquired where my basic load of rounds was the SSG yelled, "They told me not to give you any rounds, SFC!" Of course, I wanted to know who gave this order. He said the Commander and First Sergeant, and that they would be at Kandahar the next day to explain why. When they arrived, they told me that I would no longer be serving as Platoon Sergeant. My Soldiers and Platoon Leader had written statements against me saying that I had planned all along not to deploy and that they had lost trust in my ability to lead them. The reason they weren't giving me rounds was that they knew I would be upset and didn't want me to hurt anyone. Knowing all of this was complete lies, I sought out help from the Inspector General (IG). IG told me that I needed to get with my chain of command. I told them my chain of command was the problem.

At that point I felt set up and betrayed. They had brought me over to a foreign country, away from anyone who could help me, and they were trying to relieve me. So, I sought help from our higher Command. The Command Sergeant Major (CSM) for the Command we were attached to talked to my Commander and First Sergeant and informed them that they had no grounds to relieve me. He told them to reinstate me immediately. I then asked to speak with the CSM separately. I told him that I no longer wanted to work in that unit. I had lost trust in my leaders and did not feel they would protect me if I continued with them during the deployment. I was transferred to another position and placed in charge of ensuring the proper construction of kilometers of road through unknown Afghanistan territory. The position turned out to be more of a promotion. It was a high visibility job in which many high-ranking officials relied on my knowledge and expertise. God had once again used a bad situation to elevate me. He also protected me during that journey. I had to travel throughout the country and inspect different construction locations to ensure operations were going correctly. During that time, I relied on people from my old unit as well as others I did not know for transportation to the locations. That made the deployment even more stressful because many of those I traveled with often came across improvised explosive devices. I look back now and know that God's hand of protection was on me.

Finding Strength for My Journey

I had always been an avid reader of the Bible. When I was about 12 years old, I remember reading it and thinking it was like an epic storyline. I needed to draw strength from somewhere to get me through my deployment, so I began reading the Bible daily. It was amazing to me that it felt like I was reading it for the first time. It was also like I was seeing what I was reading. Much of it was what I saw in Afghanistan. The words in the Bible began to give me encouragement. There were days when I did not leave my hooch until I knew I had a rhema word from God to protect me for the day. Before I knew it, the days had flown by and the deployment was coming to an end. A lot happened during that deployment, but I found my strength to get through it.

In closing, I offer you this. The past 26 years as a female Engineer have not always been easy. The advice I give to all Soldiers and leaders is to find what gives you strength and hang on to it. Never let one person or one duty station cause you to make a premature decision to end your career. Remember the original reason why you joined. Also, when in charge, take charge. Know your worth and do not let anyone make you ashamed of it. Lastly, advice that I received at a mentorship session and now implement in my own career is to always take your seat at the table.

SERVING BEHIND THE RANK

☆ ☆ ☆ ☆ ☆

DIANE MOSLEY

The Struggle

Being a military spouse was a labor of love. Even though my husband wore the military uniform, I served also. A military spouse truly serves Behind the Rank. For my husband to serve in peace, I had to be supportive and take care of business when he was in the field or deployed. I performed the day-to-day activities. Maintaining our home became my responsibility. The military takes military readiness seriously, so training was continuously ongoing. At times, my husband would deploy or participate in field operations for days, weeks, and sometimes longer. I often thought to myself, "There has to be a better way." But, I needed to remain strong for my husband. It was enough pressure for him to leave his family, I did not need to add any more.

During the deployments or field operations, I would miss him. However, my experiences with his deployments and field operations always turned out okay. Thank God nothing ever happened during his training exercises that required me to contact him. But, I witnessed several military wives that experienced significant difficulty during their spouse's deployment or field operation.

A lot of what I saw was through my employment. At one duty station, I worked for the Army Community Services (ACS). That was my first position with the federal government. At ACS, it was our job to assist Soldiers experiencing financial difficulty with creditors. We negotiated a repayment plan with the Soldier's creditors. We assisted many wives while their husbands were in the field or deployed. It was often sad to see Soldier's serving their country and their family struggling to eat or pay their bills. My husband was an enlisted Soldier, and most of his peers' wives did not work. Since I worked, we were afforded financial freedom not readily available to most of his fellow Soldiers.

We lived in post housing, and I could often tell when the Soldiers were away on a training exercise. I would see the wives struggling to feed their children, put gas in the car, keep the cable on, and pay the telephone bill. There were multiple times when one of my husband's Soldiers' wives called me for assistance while their husband was away. The request was not significant—a ride to the store, a few dollars, watch the children, etc. The wives formed a bond and became surrogate family members. We supported each other during our spouses' field operations or deployments. It helped the time go faster.

My job was fulfilling as it afforded me the opportunity to serve a lot of military families. It gave me great pride to assist them during financial crisis, to negotiate their payment plans, and to help them create budgets. That was my way of helping with the readiness of the Army. I was diligent to follow-up with the families and the creditors to see that our plan was working. It always gave me such pleasure when we could tell families their debt was paid in full. It was a system that worked—creditors got paid and Soldiers learned the value of managing their finances properly. It meant their families would no longer struggle during periods of separation due to deployments or field operations.

The System

The system was that ACS stepped in as a third-party negotiator and the creditors agreed to contact ACS regarding payments. One of the ACS staff members would speak with the creditor and then make the necessary contact with the Soldier or the family member. If our contact revealed the Soldier's financial obligations had changed, we would renegotiate payments to allow funds for needs like food for the month, gas, etc. The goal of the ACS was to leave the Soldier and his family with enough money to fulfill their daily living needs.

Some of the cases were challenging because some of the Soldiers and their wives were young, probably away from home for the first time, and they had limited financial knowledge. But, now they were on their own trying to manage a house and all their living expenses. It was easy for them to obtain credit, but some of the Soldiers did not understand credit. I can remember one case where the Soldier kept writing insufficient checks. We assisted the Soldier in arranging a payment plan to pay the checks and fees, but he kept writing more insufficient checks. We (ACS staff) couldn't understand why the Soldier kept writing checks, so we asked him to bring in the checks. We finally had a breakthrough when the Soldier stated, "I thought I had money as long as I had checks." While the staff found it comical, it was a lack of knowledge on the Soldiers part because it was something he had never learned. We assisted the Soldier with some budget training and that took care of the issue.

I believe serving in the military is admirable, but some of the Soldiers' financial skills were not fully developed. Most of the clients we served benefited from budget and financial counseling, and most Soldiers successfully completed the program. This was truly a great and necessary program for the young Soldiers. I really enjoyed my position. Not just because it paid me a salary, but because I felt I was making a difference in the lives of military Soldiers and their family members. I believed it was commendable that the Army would fund a program to support the Soldiers with their financial concerns. And because the people I worked with were military family members, they had a vested interest in assisting the Soldier.

The Mission to Serve

After about a year of working at ACS, I was promoted to another position working in Military Finance. Even though I was not a financial clerk, I was instrumental in assisting Soldiers who experienced difficulty obtaining their pay. I worked for the Chief of Military Pay. I worked this position for about a year before I was promoted to a position in the hospital. Again, I was able to assist Soldiers and their family members.

Each job I held helped me to pass the time while my husband was in the field or deployed. My work helped me to rechannel my thoughts and made me feel as if I was making a difference in the lives of others. It made me feel like I was serving my country along with my husband. In the three positions I held, there was always a new family to assist. This was good because at this duty station my husband spent a significant amount of time in the field or being deployed. I can remember us preparing him for his multiple field operations or deployments. We would shop and purchase lots of food for him to take with him. The military provided food, MRE's (Meals Ready to Eat), but my husband did not like the MRE's. Prior to him leaving, we would go to the commissary and purchase as much food as he could carry in his backpack. Many times, he purchased more food than needed so he could share with his friends. At times I would comment, but my husband was all for assisting his fellow Soldier. He knew one of his friends struggled financially and could not afford to take money from his family to purchase food for the field, so he purchased extra food and hygiene products. Even though I did not always agree, I wanted to support him. After a while, I looked forward to clipping coupons to save on the items.

As my husband was promoted, standing Behind the Rank took on a new title. He assumed responsibility for Soldiers under him. This at times came with assisting the young Soldiers with daily living needs. My husband would get telephone calls from his Soldiers while at home. Sometimes they would interrupt our plans. I was forced to remember that my husband was a Soldier and assisting those under his command was part of the job. I had to serve too. Our life operated around the military. The military told us when my husband would go to the field. Our lives functioned around the military exercises. I did not complain. I was proud of my husband, the Soldier. However, living with a Soldier can be a true testament of love. There were times I wished my husband was at home, but he was in the field or deployed. There were times I wished we could plan activities, but he had a military function or had to take care of one of his Soldiers.

I enjoyed my life with the military. And, as a military wife, I served along with my husband. Yes, I believe I served as well; yet, my service was in silence to the military. My service was to my husband. What my jobs provided was an avenue for me to have my own identity. My jobs took me from behind my husband's rank. On my jobs, I was known by my name not "the Soldier's wife." I had no problem with being a Soldier's wife, but it was easy to lose your identity as a military wife because everything revolves around the Soldier's identity. My employment afforded me the opportunity to maintain my own identity.

I can truly say I enjoyed my military experience. It opened opportunities for travel, friendships, and new discoveries. It gave me the opportunity to support my husband while he served the country. Of course, I made some mistakes and I would do a few things differently if I had to do it over again. Looking back, I could have been a little more supportive. One thing I know for sure is that if I had to do it over again, I would still take the military life of service. I would still marry a Soldier.

As a military wife, I tried to represent my husband in a favorable way. I did not want to bring embarrassment to him. I obeyed the rules and supported him during his military functions. I supported my husband because I wanted him to advance in his military career. I was proud of him and thankful for the opportunities afforded to me by his service in the military.

One thing I would like for military spouses to take away from this chapter is to always support your husband or wife. Soldiers have an important mission. The Soldier needs assurance that his or her family is okay while they are deployed or on a field operation. Remember your years of support will pay great benefits. Military spouses and Soldiers enjoy benefits both during and after service. Even though you may not wear the uniform, the spouse serves with the Soldier. A military spouse's support is important to the welfare and benefit of your service member. Because of the sacrifices of military families, we enjoy a great freedom. Spouses, just know you are invaluable to your military Soldier even if it is never verbalized. I have spoken with multiple Soldiers and almost each one of them have voiced how much they appreciated their spouse's support while they served, especially during separations due to military training and deployments.

My wish is that something I wrote encourages the military spouse who is serving along with their spouse. Thank you for your support. We are a better nation because of your service.

LIVING MY DREAM

☆ ☆ ☆ ☆ ☆

DANNIELLE RAMOS RASH

From Rapping to Typing

People ask me how I became a military and federal resume writer, so this is my story. My name is Dannielle Ramos Rash and I am a native from "the Island," Rhode Island that is. I'm also a fourth generation military Veteran that served my country proudly, both as a service member and a federal civilian employee. Prior to joining the military at age 19, I wrote and entered a song for a drug-free contest. It won first place. I went on to record the song in a recording studio and made several rap videos for a drug-free program for schools. This was the beginning of realizing my gift for writing. Interestingly, there is no better training for writing resumes than understanding how to write a rap song!

During my military career, I served in the Army National Guard, Army Reserves, active duty, as well as the Reserve Officers' Training Corps in college. I have been employed both as a government contractor and a federal civilian employee. I joined the military and thrived in the human resources arena. My tenure in the military as a human resources manager allowed me to hone my writing and editing skills even more. I enjoyed writing and crafting poems, speeches, and resumes. I took pride in designing and creating these documents for others and ensuring that their resumes looked visually appealing. In addition, I worked with other Veterans and assisted them in achieving their civilian and federal career goals.

Having had the honor of serving my country proudly for many years and due to an extensive military background of working for a government contractor and the Department of Defense as a civilian employee, my career goals were very specific. Therefore, you can believe me when I say I totally understand what military Veterans go through when making their transition into the civilian workforce. I have literally walked a mile or two in their boots and I definitely get it! I know what works and what does not when transitioning into the civilian and federal workforce. I strive to stay on top of the latest resume industry trends which have changed dramatically over the past 10 years. I share the most recent industry trends with my clients and Veterans daily. Through my business, I have worked with military clients worldwide who are transitioning into the civilian or federal workforce.

I served proudly as a Chairborne Ranger, as the job I held in the military was an administrative specialist. I remember the recruiter asking me to perform a timed typing test. He told me I had to type roughly 25 words a minute to pass the administrative school and graduate. I took the test prior to attending the school and typed well over 40 words per minute. As the years went by, the job series changed to what we know today as a human resource specialist. In addition, I held an additional skill identifier (F5) which is a Postal Operations Clerk. I often joke with folks and tell them I went "postal" when I served in the military.

From Here to There

During my tenure in the military, I have worked with joint Military Commands to include the Army, Air Force, Navy, Marine Corps, and the Coast Guard at Kimpo International Airport in Seoul Korea, and the Military Entrance Processing Command in Louisville, Kentucky. I hold a vast knowledge of military organizations. As a proud Army Veteran who has served abroad and stateside as a military member and a civilian employee for the Department of the Army, my years in the military have well equipped me to collaborate with points of contact from numerous sources to include: The White House, Congress, military Veterans, retirees, spouses, family members, and major military commands.

I navigated a number of stateside and overseas moves to places such as: Panama, Germany, Korea, and Hawaii. In 2006, I relocated to the Washington, D.C. area and was employed at the United States Army Human Resources Command. My job there was to manage Soldiers worldwide for the Department of the Army. I mentored Soldiers and nominated and placed them in special careers to include: Drill Sergeant, recruiter duty, and other special assignments. It was at that job that I became the unofficial resume writer for my colleagues. I was the go-to person for my co-workers, reviewing their federal resumes prior to them submitting to USAJobs.

In 2010, when my federal job relocated out of state due to a base realignment and closure, I had the choice of either relocating to Kentucky or losing my position. My husband did not want to relocate from the D.C. area, so that was when I started living my entrepreneurial dream. I knew I had the perfect skillset to assist others with their resumes and job search, especially military Veterans.

During that time, my son was diagnosed with an Autism Spectrum Disorder, Sensory Processing Disorder, as well as a host of other comorbidities. Therefore, becoming an entrepreneur would assist in handling most of the childcare-related duties. So, First Class Resumes & Career Services was birthed as a small business in Northern Virginia.

I remember thinking that my greatest challenge was, "How will I stand out among all the competitors?" Since I understood military terminology, I specialized in assisting military Veterans to make the transition into the civilian workforce. However, I knew I wanted more in order to set my business apart. So, to address that challenge, I earned several certifications and specialized in Federal resume writing and federal job applications.

From Employee to Entrepreneur

So began my journey to become a professional resume writer. Over the years, I became the founder and principal writer at First Class Resumes & Career Services, a certified federal career counselor, a certified federal job search trainer, a certified professional resume writer, and a member of both the Professional Association of Resume Writers and Career Directors International. I continue to provide powerful federal resumes and career documents for job seekers (mostly military Veterans) around the globe.

I have met other professional career coaches and resume writers through joining industry associations and organizations. In addition, I have attended resume conferences to network with other writers. Yes, there is such a thing! This year, I am heading abroad to Madrid, Spain. I am taking my resume business overseas to connect with other writers, educate myself and continue to perfect my craft. This conference will be a true international experience, with career coaches joining from across the United States, Europe, Australia, South America, and beyond.

I am fortunate to have realized my passion in federal resume writing. This talent has allowed me to embrace my love of writing and build relationships that assist other military

Veterans in landing their dream job. I continue to take pleasure in bringing out the best in other Veterans and highlighting their potential, as well as maximizing their chance for obtaining an interview.

At First Class Resumes & Career Services, we assist Veterans we haven't met. It is always such a great achievement and I feel fantastic knowing that what I do daily aids them. We support our nation's Veterans with writing their resumes, gaining interview skills, creating LinkedIn profiles, and getting them that job offer! I wake up every morning knowing that my purpose in life is to help my Brothers and Sisters in Arms.

I always ask my clients if they think their resume has too much military language in it. Most of the time it does and they learn how to transform their military skills and education into a dynamite civilian resume. Since they are transitioning out of the military, it's time to get ready for the next chapter in their life—a civilian career! The most important tool in their arsenal during their job search is their resume. However, getting their military service to convert over and be understood by the civilian world can be extremely difficult.

When departing the military, Veterans have many options. And when they have the perfect resume, it can impact their life in numerous ways. The typical military transition process should be started as far out as 18 months. But, most transitioning military don't get the chance to start their transition that far in advance.

Nevertheless, if given the chance to jumpstart the transition process, I always tell my clients to take full advantage of the time to get their ducks in a row so that they are well prepared.

One of my clients had just retired as a Sergeant Major with over 20 years in the Army. He was stationed in Korea and had never applied for a federal job in his life. With my assistance, he applied for his first position and was hired. My clients typically work with me on their resume and federal application simultaneously. This particular Veteran is now working on his third federal application with me. He landed the first two positions with my assistance and I could not be more excited for him.

Military service members are under the impression that they should completely remove all things military from their resumes. However, going to this extreme can often be a mistake. There are hundreds of civilian employers that want to hire them because of their military experience. It doesn't matter if a Veteran was enlisted for four years or 20 years, they all have knowledge, accomplishments and skills. Transitioning military and Veterans need to ensure that they demonstrate their value to an employer as well as make their career documents visually appealing to the hiring manager.

Veterans have trouble explaining the value of their military experience. They often struggle in this tough job market and it makes it harder for them to obtain a professional high paying job. One of the main reasons Veterans are not getting positions is not due to them being unqualified. Instead, it is because they fail miserably at writing and creating an outstanding resume. In addition, many recruiters and hiring managers who have never served in the military have trouble understanding their military experience.

While hiring managers do appreciate their service, this rarely turns into a job offer. The best thing Veterans can do is show how they are able to add value to the organization.

From Soldier to Living My Dream

My clients often view their resumes and say, "Wow, I would hire me!!!" They also call me and are so excited that they just received a job offer, and it really brightens my day to receive that call! That moment is when I know it is all worth it and that what I do does make a difference in the lives of our nation's Veterans. I honestly feel I am changing the world, one Veteran at a time.

Here are some final success tips for our Veterans that are reading this:

1. For Vetrepreneurs: Do what you LOVE, and success will follow!

2. Flaunt it if you got it! Veterans have an extensive career background, so do not hold back. Just flaunt it, especially when you get to the interview stage!

3. Entrepreneurs and Jobseekers: Keep a positive attitude and continue to encourage yourself daily.

4. Finally, for job seekers: Stay positive, stay focused, and do not give up because you only need to hear "You are hired" one time!

I truly love what I do and am here to help and assist Veterans. If you would like advice on a civilian job search or maybe you or someone you know needs guidance through the federal employment application process and into a rewarding career in the federal service, send them to First Class Resumes & Career Services! You can visit us at: www.first-classresumes. com. If you would like a complimentary resume review, email us at: support@first-classresumes.com. And remember that we stand by our motto and promise to design and deliver dynamic resumes to win interviews by "Taking YOU HIGHER to get HIRED!"

FROM UGLY SCAR
TO BEAUTY MARK

RISE UP AND SAY YES TO YOU

☆ ☆ ☆ ☆ ☆

WANDA PETTY

Silent No More

Experiences are meant to teach and guide us to our future. However, sometimes we allow them to define who we are until the clouds are removed from our mind. There's one incident I remember like it was yesterday.

I was an E-4, married with two children, and on my second tour as dual military at Fort Carson, Colorado. No matter what time of year it was, we could expect to see four seasons (all in one day). We were just getting settled into our new townhome and familiarizing ourselves with the base. The city was desolate due to most of the units being deployed in Saudi. The crime rate had escalated, and the Soldiers who were returning were constantly fighting with each other, sometimes it ended fatally. So, Commanders had their hands full, and domestic disputes weren't given much attention. They were considered smaller problems.

My husband and I married as high school sweethearts and we were 14 years into the relationship. Infatuated with the length of our courtship, I was intrigued to hang in there as long as I could. The warning signs escalated, and our marriage was headed south. By now I'd experienced bruised ribs, black eyes, and regular visits to sick call. In my mind, if I told anyone the truth, that would mean I had failed. I needed to avoid failing because I'd spent most of my life, from the age of three, with my parents being divorced. I'd recognized the problems my siblings and I encountered without having a fatherly role model in our lives.

For years, my mother championed being the head of the house and providing for our needs. Sometimes, it was challenging for her financially. She covered her pain with a smile, but deep inside of her being I could see the loneliness. I didn't want to experience that pain. I'd always wanted to have a marriage that extended beyond the three years my mother and father had, and I was doing that. Or so it seemed. Domestic violence wasn't something people really understood back in the 90's. A woman was expected to accept domestic situations and be hush-hush. If she didn't, she was viewed as not being able to handle her affairs, and the Army made it clear that *every* Soldier should be able to handle their own matters. Otherwise, it was cause for discharge. Subsequently, I became shameful and more reserved as time went on. Anyone who knew me at work, as a neighbor, and even previous acquaintances from my first assignment could tell there was something going on. Yet, no one ever called the police, and I was quiet as a mouse. Deep down inside, I knew they could see the shift in my attitude or change of my facial features sometimes. Still, I cannot remember one person asking me, "How are things at home?" If they did, I probably covered it up with a smile saying, "It's fine."

The abuse went on for an extended period. One day, I remember gaining enough courage to say something to a close friend. She became my refuge. Several times, I attempted to share with women in my family what was happening. I expressed my feelings and sought advice; but, the response was always, "You have a good man, he's taking care of his family. Look, you have a home, an investment property, and a brand new BMW. He's even bought you a one-carat diamond ring! You don't find many men like that. Whatever it is, the two of you can work it out."

Soon, I felt there was no reason for me to say anything to anyone. They wouldn't have understood. I realized that physically I was in this all alone. If I was going to make it, I had to allow God (faith), the survival skills I'd learned from the military (intelligence techniques), and the rearing of my mother (the ability to be independent) to keep me alive. It took me a while to gain strength and use wisdom, but I had to remind myself who I am, whose I am, and accept the fact that I had become dependent upon someone else to make me whole or complete. I had placed too much trust in man to give me happiness and life.

The Turning Point

Two years later, I earned a three-day weekend pass award for exceeding 300 points on the Physical Fitness (PT) test. Now settling into a one-bedroom apartment, I decided to stain the antique headboard purchased at a yard sale and give it a fresh look. I was on my way to recruiting school. Actually, we were accepted as a couple. However, our Command didn't know we were separated because this was something we both desired to achieve in our careers. Our plan was to attend anyway, then officially separate after graduation. During the course of the day, I shared with both my best friend and my mother that I would be on my first date at the movies. I made sure they knew my whereabouts anytime I was not at my apartment.

That evening, I attended the movies with a friend. Upon arriving in the parking lot of my home, I felt watched. I saw nothing, so my date and I entered my residence. Soon after, the phone rang. I didn't answer it because I thought, "Who could be calling me at this time of the night? The two people I am accountable to know my plans." I let the voicemail accept the call. It was my husband (currently, my former husband). I knew something was strange because I heard the train passing outside of my bedroom window when the phone rang and again during the replay of his message. That meant he was close by when he called, perhaps at the 7-Eleven around the corner.

I advised my date to leave. I didn't want him to get harmed. So, he departed. Needless to say, that night was strictly a night of survival for me. God sent an angel to protect me from the stabbing wounds and other injuries that took place. I was held hostage in my own apartment until 8:00 a.m. the next morning. The only thing that saved me was him having charge of quarters duty (CQ) that Saturday morning. Upon arrival at the hospital, I was told that nothing could be done for the wounds I'd received because it was past eight hours of the injuries. I was frightened, and I knew I had to do something different. I hid at a girlfriend's home for over a week before he figured out where I was. I was able to obtain a protective order by then; but, that was not enough.

Reluctant to tell my Command what happened (I didn't want him to get in trouble or myself to receive a dishonorable discharge), I said nothing. However, little did I know, my best friend revealed the complete story to our First Sergeant (she and I worked together). I felt relieved knowing the truth was out and I no longer had to keep the secret. What shocked me the most was how it was handled by my Command. It was as if he received only a slap on his wrist. My Commander phoned his Commander and warned him to stay away from me. That was it! My life had been in a downward spiral for over two years, I had many near-death experiences, health records to prove consistent injuries, and the only thing that happened was a semi-threat? I couldn't believe I was just another number of the Command, and all that mattered was that the unit looked under control with no problems. There was only one option and it required me to trust God for what was next. I knew that if I remained in Colorado Springs, I wouldn't live to provide for my family. I had to choose life for myself and my two children.

A New Beginning

I contacted the Department of the Army and requested an assignment. Korea was available, and I accepted. Thirty days later, I was gone. I didn't know how I was going to make it through that separation. After all, we had been together for 16 years. Five of them were me being a dependent, and now I was all alone. It was something I had never experienced. We were together all of my adult life. Now, the very thing I had feared (being a single mom) was happening. I was in the position of having to perform both parental roles and I had to get myself together. I didn't know where to begin, but I had to start somewhere. I would have plenty of time to think while in Korea because the children were being cared for by both of our parents (after a while, my mother became the sole caregiver for them until I returned a year later).

I would consider that year the most profound of my life, and I began relying on God to do a new thing. I now had time to consider who I would become. There were nights I cried myself to sleep, and when I awakened my spirit was refreshed because I had released the sadness. Little by little, I was restored. In order for me to have successes, I had to reflect on where I came from. I noticed that everything in my life counts. I couldn't pass over anything because it all mattered. The way I viewed myself had to change. I had to learn to love myself before I could expect someone else to love me.

I started having a weekly Friday night date with myself. I'd sit in my barracks room and have "pamper me" nights. I gave myself pedicures, manicures, and facials while reading *Essence Magazine* and Iyanla Vanzant's books. I discovered how a woman should carry herself and meditated on what I'd read.

Up to that point, I'd gone by the instructions of the women in my family. Yep, the same women who told me, "Everything will be fine." I now had to recreate myself. And since I didn't know what to do, I decided to read the Bible and let it teach me how God desired me to be. I believe I grew closer to Him during that time. Now, He had my attention. I had nowhere to go. Many days I'd sit still or take quiet walks in the small town outside of our casern. The people knew me well. Some thought I considered myself too good to hang out, but that wasn't the case at all. I knew what I was facing when I returned home. I would have to be a single parent, and Lord knows I didn't have a clue what that would look like. I was afraid, and deep down I knew I carried faith that would hold me through the process.

When times were tough, I believed God wouldn't let me hit rock bottom. He's shown Himself worthy of my trust over and over again. Now, it's a lifestyle for me to trust Him in ALL things. I knew He had a greater plan for me because He continually provided miracles. I can see that even though this experience was traumatic, He has allowed me to have compassion for others and use it as a platform. There's no way I can explain the miracles that have happened because I learned to trust Him. As Maya Angelou once said, "When I knew better, I did better."

What I Understand for Sure

Life is comprised of experiences that are meant to catapult us to the next level. It's not about the setbacks that made us look as if we'd failed. It's about how we learned from those experiences and allowed them to guide us to our God-given purpose. We are spiritual beings having a physical experience. We are to use our light to help others who are caught up in their experience (the moment) to see the truth. We must help them find their light and how they should allow it to guide them into their purpose. I've since discovered the road to being my highest best. So, when I encounter moments of lower vibration, instead of sabotaging and judging myself, I choose to consciously acknowledge how viewing myself in that way serves me. If it doesn't, I know I'm not being my best. I believe God wants to use each of us to bring His light to those that are lost in the moment (caught up in life). We must choose to see our circumstances as lessons for our toolbox.

Today, I've taken the tools I've collected throughout the years and redefined them to serve me in a higher capacity. A capacity that can change the world by teaching other women to use their voice to fulfill their God-given purpose and create their own economy with entrepreneurship. It didn't happen overnight; it took time. A few years ago, if someone would have told me I would be contributing to the lives of others at this magnitude, I wouldn't have believed them. But, the days of me thinking I'm broken are over!

It's time for us to rise up and rightfully claim the blessed life our Father has promised us. Don't allow a label society uses to describe your situation to become the way you live your life. I'm not wounded, yet I have been wounded. I'm not broken, and I don't need fixing. I'm not a victim, but I've experienced victory. Choose to see yourself as a woman whose life experiences have given you wisdom. Proverbs 3:4 (KJV) says, "Wisdom is the principal thing… and with all thy getting get understanding." I pray that you now understand who and whose you are, and you are willing to keep moving forward.

The experiences I had along my journey were meant to help me become the woman God chose me to be. In order to be that woman, I had to step outside of my emotions and not let them define me. Because I did that, I was able to purchase my own home, marry a man who loves me beyond my imagination, and help other women find their voice. Say yes to yourself no matter the challenges before you. Life awaits you to live it. Now, go forth and prosper!

DOUBLE MINORITY STATUS

☆ ☆ ☆ ☆ ☆

DERAN YOUNG

Military Culture

Does the military hate women?

Does it foster a culture against women?

These may seem like harsh or strange questions, but some of the things I've experienced have left me to ponder these questions often. When I think about our society and the way that women are oppressed in every corner of the world, it's not hard to imagine that the military culture breeds sexism and misogyny. From the subtle and covert examples of male privilege, to the extreme of physical, sexual, and emotional abuse of women—it's all engrained in the military lifestyle and hard to ignore. Misogyny in the military can be noticed in the way many men devalue, belittle, or prejudge women based solely on the fact that they are the opposite sex. Most women in the military have learned to "fall in line" accordingly. In general, sexism shows up every day in various disguises. But, before any organization can effectively eradicate it, we must first be willing to explore and discuss some very sensitive topics and beliefs. However, as a former military mental health professional who advocated for victims of sexual assault and domestic violence, I know that issues such as these have a way of being swept under the rug in all branches of the military. In almost every case I was involved in (including my own), the women were made to believe that they were somehow to blame.

As a woman in the military, you have double the chance of being divorced and are four times more likely to experience sexual harassment or assault compared to civilian women. Could it be that the "tough" image of the military encourages its members to be hypermasculine, requiring an extra layer of brute and emotional callous for both men and women? As a therapist, I often ponder what truly attracts individuals to the military, especially those less likely to join such as women, and then even more so in the margins are black women. As a black woman, I was told I was a "double minority." I didn't really understand it until I felt it.

My interest in the military was the somewhat typical story of a girl who was raised in extreme poverty near a military base that seemed to offer a world of opportunities. I was a young lady who wrote my recruiter at the age of 15, and promptly enlisted in the military four months after graduating from high school. I was enrolled into the Delayed Entry Program because I graduated at the age of 17 and was unable to join until 18 years old. My grandmother could have signed a waiver but said she didn't want to be responsible for me being shipped off and dying. During the gap between high school and Basic Training, I fell into a period of homelessness, identity confusion, and sexual exploitation. I wish I could say that all ended when my time in the military started.

After arriving at my first duty station, I met a few friends, settled into my first work assignment, and started to figure out what it meant to be an adult. With few role models and little to no guidance, I began identifying myself through the men I attracted. There were too many to count, and each one provided me with a lesson on who I should be.

As a child who was severely abused and neglected (physically, emotionally, and sexually), so I was used to being controlled, powerless, and subservient (I explained more about this in my book, *Unchain Me Mama*). One of the Air Force core values is, "Service before self" and this was a concept that I had lived my life by for as long as I could remember. So, when I had my first wrestle with sexual harassment at work, it almost seemed like no big deal.

"Airman Young, I told that other young Airman he should date you. You are cute, kinda sexy, and you have nice tits." This was coming from my supervisor's supervisor. Of course, I was uncomfortable because he was married and old enough to be my father, but I knew my role was to play it off and pretend as though I wasn't offended at all. How could I be? That wasn't allowed. I was smart enough to know that it would only drag MY character and credibility into question. Which is what happened in a similar situation about 10 years later. Only worse.

The Struggle

Before we get to the part where things got worse, I'd like to start with happier times. The time just after I married my ex-husband and believed all my dreams had come true. I had beat the odds! Here I was a military woman, mother, and wife. I was everything society expected me NOT to be, right? But, it wasn't enough to have a degree and a successful career. I had to first be a WOMAN.

And my ex-husband never let me forget that.

I suspect that one reason military women are divorced at double the rate of their civilian counterparts is because men are not socialized to believe that a woman's career always comes second to his. This is especially true for black men. They are taught that their identity is tied to their income. Just as mine was tied to my vagina.

It wasn't long before my ex-husband, who was also college educated and a highly qualified professional, became frustrated that I was the breadwinner and that my career demanded that I work over 50-60 hours a week, leaving him to do most of the household duties. Although I always did my fair share of cooking, cleaning, and taking care of our son, there was always a sense of tension, extreme disappointment, and feeling unfulfilled on his part. I thought maybe another baby would help solidify my womanliness and keep our marriage intact, but we didn't make it to that point. His words got harsher and he became extremely resentful. Resentful enough to do what in my mind was the unthinkable.

We divorced in August 2015, just after I had received orders to go to Italy. His response when I shared the news about an assignment to Europe was, "Of course I can't go with you." So, I put my big girl panties on and relocated to Italy as a recently divorced single mom. It was tough!!! I remember a Commanding Officer once told me that seeing my struggles made her glad she had never been in a relationship that produced a child. It was as if she was telling me that my status as a single mother now made me too womanly for the military. I tried harder to find my place, to fit in, and to just go with the flow as much as possible and ride out my last five years. But, those years were cut short by an incident that occurred during my attendance at an Advanced Officer Leadership Course.

It was my first time away from my son. I had learned to bury all my feelings, frustrations, and worries into my role as a mother. But, now I was left to ask myself again for six whole weeks... Who am I as a leader? As an Officer? But, most importantly, what did I REALLY want?

The Trauma

Being surrounded by mostly male Officers and women with no "attachments" reminded me of just how different my life was. My values, priorities, and beliefs seemed so foreign to everyone else. I was like a unicorn. But, a very sad one. I cried most of the first week. I felt alienated and very much out of place, until an instructor showed special attention to me and said he wanted to support me during my time there so that I got the most out of the training. During the first extended weekend, he offered me a ride to Atlanta. I shared with him that I felt some time away might be helpful for me to clear my mind. I figured that since he was an instructor maybe he was one of the people I could trust the most. After all, my well-being was part of his job description, right?

About halfway down I-20, he asked me about my sexual history and if I had ever tried a threesome. Again, I found myself in that uncomfortable place, but tried to divert the conversation to a more appropriate topic. When we arrived in Atlanta, he insisted on walking me to my hotel room. Once we got to the room, he let himself in and I started to panic. I asked about the engagement party that he was scheduled to attend. He picked up the phone and told someone on the other line that he had a change of plans. I went into the bathroom feeling completely trapped. What could I say to turn this situation around? I recalled a conversation I had with a peer about this instructor. She had been stationed with him at a previous location and warned, "He is a little too friendly." She said, "He WILL try you, but all you have to do is say, 'No thanks.'" Those words echoed in my head as I composed myself and exited the bathroom to attempt to deal with the situation.

"No thanks..."

I guess in his mind, that only meant that I needed to be convinced. He said to me that I was taking this whole training way too seriously. The very mention of the training environment reminded me of the power and authority he had over my career. He was an instructor and I was a student. Would I be considered a bad Officer? One who wasn't a team player? Would he spread negative sentiments about me to other instructors? To my own instructor? Did I really come all this way to have this ruin my chances for career advancement?

So, I kept quiet and let him do what he wanted to do. Shortly into it, I grew sterner and said, "I don't want to do this." He said, "Just relax." At his request, I tried to just let it happen, but I couldn't. I knew this was something I simply had not chosen for myself. He said that he knew what would help—he pulled out a sex toy! I was so disgusted I could have puked. I shouted, "NO!" He got up angrily, yanked off the condom, and started to put his clothes on.

The next day, I texted him that I would find a ride back. I felt ashamed and guilty, beating myself up about what I should or could have done differently. I told one of my class-mates, but wasn't sure that I wanted to get wrapped up in a scandal in the middle of attending a course that was intended to help me get to the next level in my career. It never oc-curred to me that his actions were premeditated given how well prepared he was with his "equipment."

When I returned to my base after the training, I tried to forget what happened. I also vowed to take a break from men because I just couldn't trust myself. I didn't tell another soul until after falling into a very depressed state in July 2016. As a mental health professional, I knew that I couldn't continue to practice as a clinician with my own well-being in question. I was flown back to the US for extensive counseling with the hopes of returning shortly. However, after being probed and questioned about all the traumatic experiences in my life, I started to fall into a place of no return. A place where I could no longer lie about who I was. I could no longer deceive myself by becoming whatever anyone else wanted me to be. I started to process the memories and emotions of my experiences, and I felt empowered to hold others accountable for their role.

The Fight

I remember going to the Sexual Assault Response Coordi-nator's (SARC) office to make the report. It was one of the scariest days I'd ever had. I cried while writing out the report. Was I really about to bring another black man down? Not only was I a woman in the military, I was a BLACK woman. And I knew the prestige that black male Officers carried. The only thing that kept me moving forward with the case was knowing that he was likely still doing the same thing to other women. And the investigation found this to be true. There were many more students he had sex with before and after me. I think of them often and wonder if they struggle as much as I do with what happened. But even scarier, they might just think of it as the norm.

Going through a sexual assault case in the military can be brutal! From investigators asking me why this and why that, to them telling me that cases like *this* are hardly ever able to stand up in court. Although the military has strict rules against student and teacher interactions, it was as if I was being held responsible for his abuse of power. He preyed on students and he knew how to succeed. He knew we were vulnerable and conflicted. He was extremely calculated and had no remorse about it at all. Thankfully, I was engaged in therapy and had support to remind myself that it wasn't my fault.

When the results came back, I wasn't happy at all. I felt a wide range of emotions. I was frustrated that he hadn't lost his career the way I had and that he faced little to no public humiliation. There was also the complicated feeling of guilt I felt for being involved in another brother's downfall. At the end of it all, I engaged in 10 months of intensive therapy to reduce the feelings of blame, shame, and guilt. I grew into a woman with a clear sense of identity. I was no longer a double minority. I was not powerless, but completely empowered. I created an organization called Black Therapists Rock, where I stand alongside over 18,000 professionals who are passionate about raising mental health awareness for vulnerable populations such as women in the military. I proudly share my personal stories of healing across several stages and platforms worldwide. I've become a much stronger leader and influenced thousands to have the courage to speak their truth while boldly reclaiming their power and taking the steps toward healing, just as I did.

THE UGLY PROCESS OF GROWTH

WINNIE MOORE

I Owned It

It was July 2015, and I was toward the end of my tour as a Drill Sergeant (DS). I was experiencing what we like to call in the military short-timers attitude. I was serving as a Basic Combat Training Drill Sergeant and in the past 18 months I had trained over 2,400 of American's sons and daughters to become part of the greatest military in the world. I truly loved this job; it was my best assignment.

During my last six months, I worked at the Reception Battalion. That is where Drill Sergeants went to prepare to come off DS status and go back into an Operational Army unit. During that time, I had what I would call my "Own It" moment with the Senior Drill Sergeant (SDS). He instructed me to have all the female trainees dye their hair before they shipped out to their training. I refused.

Yes, I refused to follow that order. "Why?" you might ask? Because a week prior, I ordered two female Soldiers to dye their hair and it turned grey and started to fall out. I was horrified! Those Soldiers went to Basic Training with their hair falling out, thanks to DS Moore —ME! A female Noncommissioned Officer (NCO) in the United States Army with a solid 13 years of service under my belt who was very well-versed on AR 670-1, I might add.

The SDS told me my platoon of female trainees would not ship out, and that I would be counseled and recommended for UCMJ (Uniform Code of Military Justice) under Article 92: Failure to Obey a Lawful Order. I could not believe it! Had I done the right thing? Sometimes we do things to make life easier, at least that's what we would like to hide behind. Who wants to ruffle feathers or go against the norm? This hair dying ritual had become the norm at the Reception Battalion because many of the female DS's lacked the fight to stand up and say "No, this is wrong." I specifically remember while on DS duty receiving natural blonde female Soldiers to the unit with dark colored hair. One day, I asked one of the Soldiers, "Why did you dye your hair?" Her reply, "The DS at reception made us do it."

I had a hard time believing that my counterparts were doing this to these Soldiers. I had to find out for myself because all NCO's know that information traveling through the private news network (PNN) is not reliable at all. So, when I became an in-processing DS and discovered that female trainees were being ordered to purchase hair dye, I questioned the validity and rationale behind that order. I was told by a peer, "They aren't 'in' yet, so they will do as we say."

I held my breath at this response because I was literally in a state of shock! Really? I could not believe a Senior female DS gave me that response. She rationalized it by saying, "It's just how things are." My soul plunged to the floor and everything about being the standard-bearer fell out of my body. I was in a state of shock.

Well, I found myself at the day before ship day for these new trainees and I had a decision to make. It was inspection time for my platoon of female Troops and there were three female trainees I was specifically told MUST dye their hair because it was too blonde. Now, mind you, it was their natural color. Of course, they did not pass inspection. But I already knew that was going to happen. The Senior DS called me into his office and told me to make sure those three females dyed their hair by the end of the duty day. I replied, "No, I will not. Nowhere in the regulation does it state that they cannot go to Basic Combat Training with their natural hair color." In an attempt to strengthen my case, I even told him what happened to the other two females the week prior. SDS banged on his desk and yelled back at me, "I don't give a fuck, SSG Moore! You will do as you're told!" At that point, the dynamic of the conversation changed. I became fearful for my life and no longer felt safe in the SDS' presence. I ran out the door furiously dialing my Commander's number. No answer. I left one hell of a message! My next call was to my First Sergeant, informing him that I did not feel safe at the company, I was going home, and I would not be back unless that SDS was not in the area. I knew that was highly unlikely and perhaps even impossible.

I then got into my truck, and on my drive home the tears began to flow while memories of my abusive marriage flooded my thoughts. For years, I'd buried my pain and it took that bang on a desk to let me know that I was not healed. I had not released that hurt, nor had I moved past the beatings or the name calling in that harsh tone. No woman should be spoken to like that. For over a decade I had been pretending for everyone, even myself. The tears continued to flow heavier. I stopped driving because I had to truly own that I was a damaged woman.

But what was damaged though? Was it my ego, my self-esteem, my womanhood, my heart, or my ability to be a leader?

When I got home, my children were already there. I could not face them, so I sat in my truck in the garage until I knew they had gone upstairs. The brokenness I felt inside was unspeakable, and not even a good bottle of d'Asti could mend it. I woke up the next morning with no desire to face the day, but I heard a voice say to me, "It's time to own it." So, I asked God to give me the strength for a face to face with the SDS.

I went to work and explained to the SDS how his actions made me feel and that it triggered emotions inside of me from my abusive past. For me, as a woman, this was a pivotal moment because it forced me to OWN fear, pain, hurt, and a level of anger I'd kept buried simply because I did not want to deal with the TRUTH that someone hurt me deeply. As leaders, always use caution, especially with females, because you never know what lies dormant and can be triggered by your words or actions. At 42, I felt like owning my pain and hurt was the manifestation of growth. But, before I could truly see that growth within, I had to release the pain, hurt, and fears I had allowed to build up for years and fuel my negative attitude.

Release It

After owning that I was a damaged woman, I took 45 days of leave from the military. I used that time to look at patterns of my behavior, and my actions and attitude toward life. I asked myself these questions:

"What drives Winnie?"

"Is it anger, hurt, pain, love, pity, or does she have a point to prove?"

"What gives me purpose?"

"Why do I want to mend my brokenness?"

During that process of release, I wanted to know who I was because "Who are you?" seems to be the million dollar question. We all know the normal response given to that question is, "I'm a mom, a Soldier, a woman. I'm also strong, compassionate, nurturing, passionate, and so many other things." And yes, those wonderful adjectives can be used to describe us. But at that point, I didn't need any descriptive words. I really needed to know who I was.

I came to know who I am because of something I like to call "The ugly process of growth." During that process, I was moody because I was dealing with demons I'd kept locked away for years. To be honest, I didn't want to know the extent of my damages. But deep down, I knew it was time to repair. No more band-aids. I went back as far as I could in my life experiences to figure out if I had self-love because without that you are spinning like a hamster on a wheel. I discovered I did have self-love, but what I lacked was love from my mother. So, my journey of healing began.

Growing up in the West Indies, my grandmother raised me. My mom was never around because she left and came to America to make a better life for us. But, she forgot me for quite a while and I felt abandoned. Although I had my grandmother's love, there's just no replacing the love and comfort of a mother. When I was ten, my mother came back to Trinidad and Tobago to get me after the death of my grandmother. I was excited to come to America, but that excitement was short-lived once the sexual abuse at the hands of my stepfather began. I suffered in silence for many years. After working up the courage to tell my mom, she blamed me. She said that at 12 years old, I seduced her husband and that's why he did what he did to me.

I wondered if I should equate that situation to how love is shown by a parent or if I should equate it to how a man shows love to a woman, even though I was not a woman. When I shared the situation with a supervisor at my first job, he said it was nasty and called the police. I was removed from my mother's home and placed in foster care. And even though I had a counselor who told me every visit that it wasn't my fault, the guilt and shame had already taken root inside of me.

I needed an escape, so I took up running. The pavement never judges me. I can show up 200 pounds and it will embrace me. I can scream and tell it my deepest desires without fear of it telling others. I moved forward with my life, carrying guilt and shame with me, and became a mom at age 20. The relationship that produced my child didn't last long. Then, I got married at 24 to a physically abusive man. I didn't want to be beaten on anymore, so I sought refuge in the military. Yes, I joined to get away to a place where I could prove myself. But, who was I working to prove anything to? Even in the military I had no support, no cheering squad. It was just me, my pain, my anger, my hurt, and my disappointments.

Did I seek professional help? Yes and no. Because I was afraid of the stigma that came with seeking professional counseling as well as the impact it could have on my career, I used an outside source called Military One Source. They provided me with a therapist who gave me the tools to use in the release process. I declared to myself that I didn't just want to relive my pain and talk about it, I wanted to release it and be FREE. I felt like I was carrying dead weight most days. For me to truly grow and become who I knew in my heart I was supposed to be, I needed to release those demons. I started volunteering at a domestic violence shelter, and I came face to face with my bruises many times. I spoke to women that were survivors of abuse, and in listening to their stories I knew I didn't want to give my abuser that kind of power over me anymore. The only way to break free was to give it to God.

I purchased a full-length mirror, stood in front of it every day, and with my head held high stated words of affirmation, love, and compassion. I exhibited greater self-love and focused on being a better person by just letting go of all those things that weighed me down and hurt my soul. I vowed to be more compassionate and understanding to others. I told myself that I would be more giving and open to change. Once I started doing that, I felt a weight lift off me. Don't get me wrong, there are times when people take advantage of me, yes, but I give those situations over to God because He can handle them better than I can. I often ask myself, "Is the release worth it? Is my pain over?" My response? "Yes, it's worth it. And, nope, it's not over because every day I'm releasing something else." Why? Because I want to be free. I want to continue to grow. Knowing when it's time to release is the key to moving forward. I now realize that if I had never had that encounter with that Senior Drill Sergeant, it is likely that I never would have taken the steps to heal or grow from the hurt and pain of my past.

Growth

After I released all that pain, hurt, and misguided anger, there was only one thing left to do—grow from it of all, become a better me, show off a new attitude, and smile more with my newfound boldness. I share my story of surviving abuse with women every opportunity I get because I want them to know it's okay to be angry; but, you must know when it's time to let go and move forward. Growth is never just for yourself, it's for those around you as well. I say this because our children are a product of the environment we create. If we don't release our past hurts, it will affect them. I knew I had to break my cycle of pain due to a lack of my mother's love by showing my daughter unconditional love when she became a teenage mother at 17 years old. Although I was disappointed, I would not turn my back on her. I embraced her and said, "We are in this together."

My growth process continues. Raised voices no longer bring me to a place of fear. I'm okay with speaking my truth and not concerned about being judged. For the first time in my life, I'm not living by rules other than the ones I've created for myself, which are: stay in a place of ever learning and never give negative people space in your mind because they aren't paying rent to live there.

IDENTITY CRISIS

☆ ☆ ☆ ☆ ☆

BRIGETTE MCCOY

Self-Identify

As I look back over my life, I recognize there have been at least three times of significance where I needed to figure out who I was. The deeper questions of "What do I stand for?", "What are my core values?", and "What do I want my legacy to be?" required me to seriously reflect at different points in my journey.

In the fall of 1991, I saw a woman Naval pilot testify on TV that she had experienced sexual assault at the hands of the men she served with. At that time, I felt my stomach clench and lightheadedness touched me. For a moment I thought I would either throw up or pass out from hearing those words out loud in a public place. I had not spoken of my experiences in the military and came to realize that my narrative would have elements closely aligned with what was being described on television. I examined her face as a camera went in for a close-up and wished her the best. It would be some 20-odd years before I would trade places with her and be the face on the camera. There would be a six-year period that I would stand up in front of the media and anyone who would listen to tell about the experiences that shaped my life and negatively impacted me for decades. It would be a total of two decades before I would recognize myself as a Veteran and examine how my service changed the trajectory of my life.

My hopes were to stay in the military. I had no plans to leave the service, I only planned to attend Primary Leadership Development Course (PLDC) when the war was over in preparation for my next promotion. But here I was, fearing for my safety and being pressured to sign papers to get out of the military following a reported sexual harassment incident. My future and identity were tied to the military and what I could achieve within the ranks. Unfortunately, my plans to have a long military career and impact military history were shattered by the orders to ETS (Expiration of Term of Service). I left the military during the first week of April 1991, it was the middle of the Gulf War.

After my ETS, being a Veteran for me only meant getting job credits for hire, applying for the GI Bill, and gaining a VA loan. In no other circumstances in the 1990's did I find a need to "self-identify" as a Veteran, especially being a woman who had not retired from the military. The only reason I connected with the VFW was because they were assigned to my claim for my back and asthma which was awarded zero percent. No one explained to me that my initial claim was just the start and I should keep pursuing. No one was there to direct me on how to file a claim for the injuries I sustained due to harassment and assault. At the time, I had never heard of military sexual trauma (MST). The first person to say the words out loud to me was woman Veteran advocate, Susan Avila Smith, during a discussion in 2007 about homelessness and women Veterans. The next time I would hear the words would be alongside the mental health term Post Traumatic Stress Disorder (PTSD).

Self-Denial

After years of silently struggling, including episodes of homelessness, an unsuccessful marriage, and anxiety that grew into agoraphobia, I went to the VA out of desperation and in extreme crisis. I was screened at my initial visit for military sexual trauma and sent to a mental health counselor. I was hurt, embarrassed, and extremely anxious. At times, I didn't even make it to individual appointments and group counseling sessions until they were over. Other times, I attended group sessions where I wept and vomited intermittently the entire 90 minutes. When I could speak at all, it was through clenched teeth and with angry words about my perpetrators enjoying their life without consequences while I was the one suffering.

Going to counseling for me was more difficult than the ETS. It challenged everything I thought about myself and who I wanted to be. During one of the sessions, the doctor stated the PTSD diagnosis. It was the first time that PTSD had been tied directly to my assault in the military. I stopped in the middle of sobbing when she said PTSD. I was adamant that there was nothing "wrong" with me and I was just experiencing prolonged sadness and needed resources to get my life back on track. To prove me wrong, the doctor assigned me to a social worker to help me sign up for resources for myself and my daughters. I applied for HUD-VASH (housing), vocational rehabilitation (educational), and filed a claim with Veterans Benefits Administration for pension benefits. Despite the assistance and resources, the sadness, anger, and despair remained. Some days it was hard to get out of bed or even look at myself. I did not want a clinical diagnosis. Just thinking about it made me angry and uncomfortable. I was worried that a PTSD diagnosis would hinder future employment opportunities. I was worried I would be denied medical insurance. I was especially worried that if anyone found out, my children could be taken away from me. I was worried about a lot of things. Many of the worries were legitimate, but so was the diagnosis. I didn't want either to be true.

It took me over a year of continuously trying group counseling, prolonged exposure therapy, taking medications, and working hard to get my life on course. There was a two-year period where I was at the VA hospital dealing with aspects of receiving VA benefits or being seen by a social worker nearly every day. It was an every hour, every day endeavor. I was in the middle of a divorce and staying on my friend's daybed. I cried a lot. I was experiencing emotional bankruptcy. It didn't help that I also had fibromyalgia, crippling lower back and hip pain, and I was taking 20-30 pills a day. Everything from high blood pressure, pain, and psych meds to vitamins and minerals. I started having the symptoms of agoraphobia. It was extremely difficult, emotionally, to leave the house. Out of necessity, a friend became my caregiver. She had to almost drag me out of the house for shopping or events. Instead of taking a break and allowing myself to get better, I continued my enrollment in college online. My focus was on gaining employment because I thought having my career and permanent employment was the identity I had left to hold on to.

Self-Identity

It took several months to finally get things going at the VA. I was awarded VA pension benefits, which in turn helped me have the income to get awarded a HUD voucher. This gave my daughters and I the opportunity to move into our own apartment. Vocational Rehabilitation's Independent Living Program was approved, and I was awarded durable medical aides to help me have a better quality of life at home and the technology needed to connect to the online community. For the first time in a long time, I looked forward to my life taking a new path and I no longer struggled with identifying myself as a Veteran. I had in many ways come to embrace that part of my identity and understood that it was a major part of my life that I could not ignore. I said it with pride and was not ashamed of being a Veteran or going to the VA for my medical care. By 2010, being a Veteran was enmeshed into every part of my life. The year prior, I started an online group for women Veterans. The group grew quickly and I was working toward forming it into an organization. I also had a support group I was connected to through VA counseling, and I was settling into my new apartment.

However, I was not prepared for what would happen next. My apartment was broken into while I was in group counseling. This caused an emotional setback for me and I soon feared living there. Within a month or so, I was evicted because there was a financial problem with the Housing Authority of Dekalb County making their contractual payments. I needed to move because I didn't feel safe in the apartment anymore and now I had no choice because I was being evicted. That meant that I had to search all over again for an apartment that would take a Section voucher in a supportive school district for my daughter where I would feel safe. That was a lot to take on in a 60-day window. I didn't think I was strong enough or had it in me to go through it all again. It was a lot to manage. I struggled desperately not wanting anyone to know what I was going through. I didn't want anyone else to worry while I worried every day. It was not easy, but I learned to pace myself and take the process day by day. I also learned that many limiting factors were impacting me and my success. I stayed inside the proverbial box so long it began to collapse on all sides. My only fear greater than leaving the box was dying inside of it. So, I had to push myself beyond my fears. I would find a new apartment to live in and work on beating the agoraphobic symptoms of PTSD.

I merged my need for camaraderie and my need to travel by attending various events across the country and meeting other women Veterans. By 2010, I was attending retreats, conferences and stand downs; hosting meetups; and I was involved with *Service: When Women Come Marching Home*, a documentary about women Veterans. The film was screened at Disabled American Veterans locations across the country as panels of women Veterans spoke about their experiences in the military. Between 2011-2013, I testified before Congress and stormed the Hill on topics related to MST and women Veterans. Everything about me had become a walking encyclopedia on women Veterans' topics. I was collaborating with dozens of organizations. I was also sitting on volunteer boards for non-profits, and city and county government agencies. I still do volunteer work for many of those organizations. In the process, the community for my organization, Women Veteran Social Justice Network, grew time and time again. We hosted retreats in Georgia and South Carolina and had conferences at Georgia Tech and Kennesaw State Universities with live streaming of women Veteran workshop facilitators and keynote speakers. At one point, it was difficult to know where the advocacy ended and I began.

I delayed medical treatments so that I would be well enough to host our events and make sure our Veterans were receiving what they needed. Although I was a Veteran, I neglected my own needs and did not place demands on other organizational leaders and programs for their support of me. Many times, even if offered, I did not accept help but passed it forward to someone else. Every moment, every dollar, every thought was on making the community better and supporting others. I struggled thinking, "If I am not an advocate and community leader, who am I?" It was a question I would ask myself more than a few times as I searched my heart for the reasons I started the work in the first place. I knew that the answer was, "To connect with a community of my peers." My initial intent and simple emotional plea was to connect and belong to a tribe. I knew what the words were, but the hard part was establishing for myself what that looked like for me, not based on any other person's idea. I didn't realize then that every experience I went through would one day help me to coach and empower others in the community.

Self-Realization

As military women, we chose that we would lay down our lives for people we would never know, never meet, and never share the same ideologies or even lifespan with. We determined it to be our calling that we would extend our lives to become links in the everlasting chain of warriors forever marked with the Seal of Service. We cannot forget who we are, who we will always be even after our deaths. No one can take from us or diminish the memory of what we have accomplished. History will only reveal the magnitude of the strength we held and the compassion we yielded to the world, even when the world didn't know it needed us.

In late 2015, I came to the realization that for some time I had limited my world to only the things related to Veterans and speaking up for Veteran women's rights. Every conversation and activity I was involved in had some connection or benefit to the women Veterans' community. My acceptance of my Veteran status had become a limited liberation. I had not cared for and accepted the other parts of my identity that are as meaningful and identifiable— mother, civic leader, woman of faith, singer, executive, daughter, lover, and friend. It would take much reflection and a lot of self-care to become aware of how I had limited myself. I began to take opportunities that expanded my community and my world view.

On one of those opportunities, I met Senior Leaders of the Gwichi'in Tribe in Alaska. I also experienced the Arctic National Wildlife Refuge during a seven-day rafting and camping expedition with the Sierra Club and several conservation focused leaders. Those experiences shifted my perspective on my identity and my place and importance in this world. My Veteran status gained a new significance based on the strengths and value of service balanced with the importance of what I have learned from my life's challenges and obstacles. My struggles helped to build my character and gave me the tools needed for future, more intense challenges. I realized that even with disabilities, I have so much to contribute beyond the experiences of brokenness. There are many elements of my identity that make me the indomitable woman I am today. Going forward, I am embracing all of me in everything I do so that when anyone asks me to identify myself, I get to do that as me, BriGette.

ABOUT THE AUTHORS

Lila Holley is a combat Veteran, a retired US Army Chief Warrant Officer Four, and the multiple award-winning, Amazon bestselling visionary author behind the Camouflaged Sisters book series. Lila partners with other courageous military women and women Veterans to share their stories of success in the military despite facing challenges along their journey.

Lila is on a mission to empower military women and women Veterans to take back the narrative and ownership of their stories. She believes there is no one better to tell these stories than the women who lived them. Lila has created multiple media platforms for women to share their stories and celebrates military women and women Veterans through her online radio show, bi-annual online magazine, virtual and live events, as well as her multiple book projects. The Camouflaged Sisters growing online community is where military women connect with each other, access resources, and share their stories.

Learn more at camouflagedsisters.com

Marsha S. Martin shares a journey that took her from a pity party victim to the victorious "Game Changer." Incarceration in a US Military Correctional Facility became her catalyst for true freedom. During her confinement, she obtained Godly direction through Bible study and connections with spiritual mentors and coaches.

Since her release in 2011, Marsha has developed programs and opportunities impacting women of all ages with messages of enlightenment, empowerment, and encouragement for their spirit, soul, and body. To impart the message of hope, she directs a local Empowerment Prayer Band Ministry. She also launched Pearls Book Club and I am the Game Changer.

As the mother of three beautiful young ladies and a grandmother, Marsha is inspired to live life abundantly. She has written several published articles and speaks at motivational and empowerment seminars. She is excited to soon release her first book: *The Birthing of the Game Changer*.

To connect, email her at marsha.martin74@gmail.com

Jacqueline Nicole Tyes is a native of Buffalo, New York, but currently resides in Charlotte, North Carolina. She obtained a bachelor's degree and a master's degree both in education from D'Youville College. Jacqueline honorably served in the United States Navy for three years before being medically discharged. She then went on to serve as an educator for 17 years until she retired in 2015. Jacqueline currently serves as an advocate for Veterans with the Disabled American Veterans, where she became the first female Commander for the state of North Carolina in June of 2016. Jacqueline was one of 10 Veterans who received the national Victories for Veterans award in June 2017. Her goal as an author is to publish books that will enlighten, encourage, and empower people of all ages and give them a lifelong love for reading, learning, and self-improvement.

To connect, email her at jnicolet2014@gmail.com

Leslie M. Dillard, a preacher's kid from Alabama, is an author, motivational speaker, spoken word artist, and playwright stationed at Fort Leonard Wood, Missouri. She officially retired from the Army in March 2018 after 35 years of service. Leslie amassed numerous awards and accommodations while serving, works in several ministries within her church, and is in training for the ministry.

She has a bachelor of science in business, masters' degrees in emergency management and strategic studies, and is working on a doctorate in strategic leadership. Leslie published *From the Situation to the Destination, Poems and Meditations to Provide Encouragement for Life's Tough Times* in November 2016. As the CEO and founder of God First Productions LLC, Leslie develops and presents works to inspire her audiences to dream big and to push to achieve those dreams—motivating them to soar!

Learn more at
www.facebook.com/GodFirstProductions

Edwina O. Freeman served in the United States Air Force from 1986-2007. She is currently employed with the Department of the Air Force as a financial management analyst at Eglin Air Force Base, Florida. Edwina is a magna cum laude graduate of Grantham University where she earned a bachelor of science degree in business administration. She is also a graduate of the DRW Coaching School and the Fibrofit Wellness Institute where she earned certifications as a holistic emotional intelligence coach and a fibromyalgia coach/ educator. She was featured as a guest speaker at the 2016 Emotional Intelligence Symposium in Orlando, Florida.

A rising entrepreneur, Edwina founded Eximius One, LLC in 2015. Her goal is to help clients who suffer from chronic illnesses achieve their desired level of physical, emotional, and spiritual wellness despite the challenges they face.

Learn more at www.eximiusonellc.com

Latisha Wilson is an Army Veteran, licensed counselor, CCI minister, author, public speaker, wife, mother, and grandmother residing in Killeen, Texas. She currently works as a transition readiness liaison, assisting transitioning Soldiers, Veterans, and family members. She's a PhD student at North Central University and a recent graduate of TAMUCT with a master of science degree in marriage and family therapy. Latisha is a member of Delta Sigma Theta Sorority Inc. and the proud founder and CEO of Narrations of Life Counseling Services, LLC.

Latisha is committed to her goal of empowering others and being a positive influence around the world through her speaking, counseling, coaching, and mentorship. Her personal quote is: "Write the story your life tells." Her favorite Scriptures are: 2 Timothy 3:16-17 and Psalm 91, as a covering for our families, the body of Christ, and Soldiers serving at home and abroad.

Learn more at narrationsoflife.com

Lee Ann D. Davis retired after serving 22 years in the United States Armed Forces. Lee Ann holds an MBA; however, her lifetime goal is to break the stigma of mental health care by making others aware of the importance of self mental health checks. She is currently in the process of completing a master of science in clinical mental health counseling. What motivates her most is being able to serve others while giving back to her community.

Lee Ann stays active by volunteering with many organizations that support mental illness and the equality for the betterment of women.

To connect, email her at leeannddavis@gmail.com

De'Meatrice "Dee Dee" Hodges enlisted into the US Army after graduating high school. While serving on one of her many deployments in support of Operation Iraqi Freedom, she was wounded in action, earning her the coveted Purple Heart Medal. Dee Dee medically retired in June 2009 due to health reasons. Now, she sings around the world.

Dee Dee's first album, *Presence of the King*, is available on iTunes, CD Baby, and other outlets where music is sold. She resides in Killeen, Texas, with her husband Michael and daughter, Jelecia.

Learn more at deedeehodges.com

Janet Williams was born in Greenville, South Carolina. She joined the Army in May of 2006 as a motor transport operator and in 2010 she was commissioned as a Second Lieutenant Quartermaster Officer. Currently, Janet remains on active duty as a logistician, serving as a Maintenance Troop Commander for the Regimental Support Squadron, 3d Cavalry Regiment.

In December 2017, Janet enthusiastically embarked on the journey to become a published author by releasing the book, *Power of Agreement*, with her mother and three sisters. She is excited to be in the Camouflaged Sisters family as one of the newest co-authors in *Behind the Rank, Volume 2*.

Tiffani K. Patterson is a RIMS AVID program specialist who graduated from San Diego State University with a bachelor of science in business management and a California Multiple Subject Teaching Credential after serving in the United States Coast Guard for 9 years (1995–2014). Her and her four older sisters were raised in Lemon Grove, California, by their father (a Navy SKCM) and mother (a teacher).

During Tiffani's time in service, she was stationed in Yerba Buena Island, California; Bodega Bay, California; Charleston, South Carolina; Georgetown, South Carolina; and San Diego, California. She was also involved in various notable Coast Guard missions on the Pacific Coast.

Tiffani believes that, "Growing into your own shoes is a part of leaving your footprint on life."

To connect, email her at tiffanikpatterson@gmail.com

Deia R. Aubrey has 28 years of active duty service in the Army. She leads combat engineers on the battlefield and serves as senior enlisted advisor and subject matter expert on leadership decisions pertaining to engineer missions. Her educational background spans from construction technology to human resource management. Her military career is comprised of a diverse mix of tactical experience, from several combat deployments to technical knowledge, that has given her a broad base from sexual harassment and assault certification to equal opportunity advisor.

Deia is a senior mentor for her organization's chapter of the Sergeant Audie Murphy Association. She is an avid volunteer and is strengthening community relationships through volunteering at local school mentorship programs. When not in uniform, Deia is behind the camera running a small photography business where the motto "Capturing the Infinite Moments" is also her mantra in life.

Learn more at aubreyphotography.zenfolio.com

Diane Mosley is a friend, teacher, and international speaker for both professional and church groups. She has always had a passion for helping others. Currently employed by the federal government, Diane is a former Sunday School secretary, superintendent, and mentor with the Atlanta Public School System.

Dannielle Ramos Rash is the founder of First Class Resumes & Career Services. Dannielle provides federal resumes for Veterans around the globe. She has been featured in the "Military Transition" chapter of *Modernize Your Job Search Letters: Get Noticed... Get Hired* and co-authored the book *Mastering Your Career Journey: 11 Career Experts Unveil the Secrets to Success.*

Dannielle has written civilian and federal resumes for thousands of military Veterans and has been coined a "Resume Goddess" by her clientele. Recently, she was hand-selected as a Veteran advisor for the Job Search Master Class™ for Veterans for over 50 Veterans in the Microsoft Software & Systems Academy. She is Camouflaged Sisters resident expert on federal resumes and the federal hiring process, a contributor in *Forward March Magazine* since conception, and she has been featured in *Women Who Served Magazine.*

Learn more at www.first-classresumes.com

Wanda "Sistah Soldier" Petty is an inspirational speaker, a God-fearing creative thinker, and a serial entrepreneur. She is the creator of SHE VET iNC. Media Productions, the founder of The National Resource Society for Women Veterans, Inc., host and visionary producer of SHE VET iNSPIRES television show, and senior recruiter of SHE WORKS Digital providing project management recruitment and virtual training. She has a background as a human resources manager, trainer, and recruiter with 21 years of active duty service in the Army. Wanda is passionate about helping women, service members, and Veterans remove barriers that attempt to stunt their personal and professional development.

Wanda is a published author of *A Spirit Warrior's Mindset: Life Mastery Series* and *The Art in Me: Unleash Your Uniqueness Through the Power of Creativity.* As a spirit warrior, Wanda is committed to eradicating unemployment and creating diversity in the working world.

Learn more at shevetinspires.com

Deran Young is a licensed psychotherapist and founder of Black Therapists Rock! She obtained her master's in social work from the University of Texas and holds a master's in public administration (with emphasis on leadership, diversity, and organizational culture). She has visited over 32 countries and conducted her final semester of grad school while establishing a high school counseling center in Ghana, West Africa.

Black Therapists Rock (BTR) is an organization of individuals and agencies committed to improving the social and psychological well-being of vulnerable communities. Deran was acknowledged by the mayor of Baltimore for "helping to educate the public on mental illness and end the stigma that is often associated with it." She has been featured in *Rolling Out Magazine* and was listed as one of the "10 Black Female Therapists You Should Know" in the *Huffington Post*.

Winnie Moore is a native of Trinidad and Tobago that came to America at age 10. She lived in Brooklyn, New York, until she joined the military in May 1999. Winnie went to Basic Combat Training at Fort Jackson, South Carolina, and then to Fort Sam Houston in San Antonio, Texas, for Advanced Individual Training. Winnie is active duty Army currently stationed at Fort Hood, Texas, with a total of 15 years in the military—11 active duty and 4 years Reserves. She has deployed twice to Iraq and once to Afghanistan and has held many leadership positions most of her military career.

Winnie has three children: a girl, Lenise, and two boys, Deron (19) and Jaden (10). She is also a grandmother of three beautiful girls. Winnie is a member of the PTA at her sons' school and volunteers at the AER food pantry on Fort Hood.

BriGette McCoy is founder and CEO of Women Veteran Social Justice Network (WVSJ). She also serves as the Atlanta Commission on Veterans Affairs vice chair, a Protect Our Defenders advisory board member, and she served as a US Army data telecom specialist during the Gulf War. BriGette uses technology for civic engagement and community building and consults Kennesaw State University to produce live streamed and on-demand broadcasted Veteran's programming.

BriGette was featured in the documentary, *SERVICE: When Women Come Marching Home*, and has been interviewed by *CNN*, *Good Morning America*, and many print and online media outlets. A highly requested conference host and keynote speaker, *The Atlanta Journal-Constitution*, *Atlanta Creative Loafing*, and *Interfaith Broadcast Atlanta* have brought her story of resilience to the community.

BriGette holds a bachelor of science in psychology, a master of theology in pastoral care, and has completed master's level courses in education media design technology.

Learn more at brigmccoy@me.com

1. TAKE A PHOTO

Take a pic of you with a Camouflaged Sisters book.

2. CAPTION IT

Tell us what you thought of the book.

3. TAG IT

Tag us @CamouflagedSisters and Hashtag it up #BehindtheRank #SilentNoMore and of course

#CamouflagedSisters

INSTAGRAM

BOOK

REVIEW

Visit us at
camouflagedsisters.com

CREATING DISTINCTIVE BOOKS
WITH INTENTIONAL RESULTS

We're a collaborative group of creative masterminds
with a mission to produce high-quality books to position
you for monumental success in the marketplace.

Our professional team of writers, editors, designers,
and marketing strategists work closely together to ensure
that every detail of your book is a clear representation
of the message in your writing.

Want to know more?
Write to us at info@publishyourgift.com
or call (888) 949-6228

Discover great books, exclusive offers, and more at
www.PublishYourGift.com

Connect with us on social media

@publishyourgift

CPSIA information can be obtained
at www.ICGtesting.com
Printed in the USA
LVHW081318040122
R17100800001B/R171008PG707518LVX00001B/1